MW01289909

EPISTLE to the AMERICANS II

What you don't know about American History

Copyright © 2009
by
David E. Robinson

Maine-Patriot.com
3 Linnell Circle
Brunswick, Maine 04011

maine-patriot.com

EPISTLE to the AMERICANS II

"Thus speaketh the Lord God of Israel, saying, Write thee all the words that I have spoken unto thee in a book." — Jeremiah 30:2.

EPISTLE to the AMERICANS II

"When the righteous are in authority, the people rejoice, But when a wicked man rules, the people groan." — *Proverbs 29:2.*

EPISTLE TO THE
AMERCANS
II
CONTENTS

Afterword

Final Word

EPISTLE to the AMERICANS II

EPISTLE
TO THE
AMERICANS
II

PREFACE - *from* EPISTLE I

D AVID, a servant of Jesus Christ by the will of God, unto the believers in the American Republic.

2 Grace be unto you and peace from God our Father, and from the Lord Jesus Christ; I thank my God upon every remembrance of you.

3 Each year, millions of Americans scramble to meet the Internal Revenue Service's deadline for filing income tax returns.

4 Think about the millions of hours of productive time these forms waste.

5 Think about the outrageous intrusion into the personal affairs of Americans these rules cause.

6 Think about the inherent unfairness of a tax system that applies different standards to different people based on their income.

7 Think about the government's unspoken threat of force and violence and terror that accompanies this process.

8 Think about how little Americans have to say about the current tax system today.

9 Think about how government wastes, misuses and illegally redistributes the revenue it collects.

10 Think about how the system confiscates your wealth before you even see it, by forcing employers to do the government's dirty work.

11 Think about how some people are forced to pay up to 45 percent of their income to the government.

12 Think about how little Americans know — or could possibly know — about a tax code written by lawyers *for* lawyers, encompassing thousands of pages that few could digest in a lifetime of study.

13 Think about how almost 50 percent of the American people have been dropped completely from the tax rolls, while the other half is forced into indentured servitude.

14 Think about how our confiscatory tax system has forced millions of homes to send both

parents into the workplace and turn their kids over to be wards of the state schools and MTV.

15 Think about how Americans are conditioned to accept all this blindly, like sheep led to slaughter.

16 Think about all this, not just today, but every day of the week.

17 It's past the time for Americans to wake up, rise up and say "No more; enough is enough; we demand our government back!"

18 It's time for a new declaration of independence; it's time for rebellion; it's time, frankly, to revolt; it's time to just say, "No."

19 You may say, *"There just aren't enough Americans angry about this injustice, this servitude to government, this slavery.*

20 *"Americans are too comfortable, with their two television sets and two cars in the garage.*

21 *"They are not going to rise up angry and take their government back any time soon."*

22 You might be right.

23 But then again recall this: the patriot movement in 1776 was a minority cause; there were far more colonists who thought life under British tyranny was more than tolerable.

24 Being informed is the first step to achieving and maintaining freedom; only an educated and moral people can aspire to be free.

25 Some people are fighting back — instead of just protecting themselves by careful financial and tax planning — by actually challenging the government directly, in an effort to overturn the entire system; some Americans are challenging the IRS and the token 16th Amendment."

26 What's different about these statements?

27 Virtually everything else that is available on this subject is either one-sided activist argumentation, or establishment propaganda based on press releases by the IRS.

28 This ground breaking report is neither.

29 Perhaps not for the first time, here is an in-depth, critical, journalistic examination of the Income Tax, the 16th Amendment, the IRS and the legal strategies employed by those fighting "the system."

30 Much effort and research have gone into this report.

31 Your money — and life — are controlled by America's banking "system."

32 There is a reason for the deliberate dumbing down of America's public schools, the "drug war," and the persecution of Christians in the U.S., and more.

33 Perhaps Americans don't want to read these kinds of reports; they say they only want to be entertained; they say this is radical; they say it demands too much change; they say they don't care about what's right or wrong.

34 But they are wrong.

35 There is a growing resistance to tyranny by insurgents.

36 Reports like this one will not only help inform the American people, but will light the fuse of a new revolutionary spirit in this country — one that will help us to throw off our shackles and rekindle liberty's fire.

37 Why not strive to be free?

38 May the grace of our Lord Jesus Christ be with you all. Amen.

CHAPTER 1

ONE of the episodes of a popular TV show, "Little House On The Prairie," portrayed a sharp avaricious neighbor of the Ingalls family pulling a raw business deal on a young man who wanted to get a small farm going so he could marry Laura Ingalls.

2 The land included a small stream originating on the seller's farm. After the young man had made a down payment and worked hard all spring to put in a good crop, the seller cut off the stream of water.

3 This not only threatened the growing crop but made the farm useless to the new owner.

4 The seller then offered to buy the land back, including the crop, for a mere $100, a fraction of what it cost.

5 When Mr. Ingalls challenged this deceitful and conniving neighbor for pulling such a crooked deal on the hopeful trusting young man, the shrewd neighbor replied, "Well... that's Business!"

6 The audience enjoyed it when Mr. Ingalls wound up and delivered a fistful of righteous indignation directly to the sneaky neighbor's jutting jaw.

7 The point is, sometimes deceitful things are done in the name of "Business."

8 CHEATING AND ROBBING IN THE NAME OF "BUSINESS"

9 Robbery is defined as "taking property from another by threat, force, or violence."

10 When this is done by a hijacker or mugger it is judged to be a felonious crime with stiff penalties.

11 But when robbery is done by manipulating circumstances within the technicalities of the law, some people — as in the above case — call it "business."

12 Of course, it is NOT business in the ethical sense of the word because legitimate business, as described by Adam Smith, is a transaction where both parties feel they have improved their position.

13 Business which amounts to "legal robbery" is really a very dirty business.

14 This happens whenever a person with a technical advantage "legally" robs another under the threat of using the force

of the courts to support his so-called "rights" in carrying out a deceitful deal.

15 We mention this simply because this has been the tragic and unfortunate history of the privately-owned "central banking business" during the past 300-400 years.

16 DIFFERENT KINDS OF BANKS

17 Banks ordinarily represent depositories for the people's savings.

18 This accumulated capital then becomes available for loans to buy farms, build homes, construct factories, and do a multitude of other things which are indispensable to a prosperous industrial society.

19 Banks, therefore are very important, and represent the major source of investment capital needed to promote the growth of a nation and provide millions of new jobs for our ever-increasing population.

20 But then there is a different kind of bank, a sort of super-bank, which represents far larger deposits of accumulated wealth. This type of bank is often referred to as a country's "central" bank.

21 Even though each bank of this type is privately owned, it often carries the name of the country it serves because the government of that country uses it as the depository for government funds, and borrows the money it needs from it in times of great emergency.

22 This privately-owned central bank therefore becomes the manager of money and credit for the entire nation. It handles major investments in agriculture, industry, factories, and homes.

23 This private central bank also loans the government the funds it needs in time of war, or for the preparations of war, and for the armaments of the nation.

24 The managers of central banks are in a powerful position to manipulate the affairs of a country for good — or evil.

25 CENTRAL BANKS SUFFER FROM TWO EVILS

26 When the managers of the central bank of any particular country are looking around for ways to accumulate even more wealth, they're tempted by two things which are inherently evil and totally destructive to civi-

lized countries.

27 One temptation is to encourage an involvement in war, so that the nation will be forced to borrow heavily from the banks.

28 Government Bonds (Government IOU's paying substantial interest) are considered to be the most valuable form of collateral for a central bank.

29 The other temptation is to promote cycles of 'booms and busts.' This consists of starting a boom with generous loans at low interest rates and after a few years suddenly raising the interest rates and calling in the loans, bankrupting home-owners, industries, farmers, and millions of people who had placed their trust in the bank to continue its policies.

30 Some economists — including Karl Marx, claimed author of the *Communist Manifesto* — want Americans to think that these boom and bust cycles are an inescapable characteristic of a free-market economy.

31 But the truth of the matter is that these boom and bust cycles are primarily a phenomenon of manipulated economics engineered by individuals who find themselves in an extremely powerful position to control money and credit but lack the moral integrity to resist the opportunity to fleece the common people who place their trust in them.

32 Any study of central banking will disclose the highly visible profile of these two pernicious problems with which central banking has been continually involved over the years.

33 It is easy to see, when pointed out, that wealthy money managers have a strong proclivity toward both war-mongering and manipulating cycles of booms and busts.

34 Having personally passed through several of these wars and cycles of booms and busts, this writer has been ever on the lookout for trends that might signify a repeat performance of this dishonest and abusive use of power.

35 LATEST BANKING INVENTION: MAKING MONEY OUT OF NOTHING

36 Several hundred years ago the goldsmiths of Europe needed to build vaults of substance for their precious metals.

37 As might be expected, it wasn't long before others asked to leave their gold in these spe-

cial vaults for safekeeping.

38 The goldsmiths consented, and gave each depositor a certificate which could be used to reclaim his precious gold at any time.

39 These certificates were therefore considered "as good as gold" and soon circulated in business channels as though they were gold.

40 In fact, they were so much more convenient to handle than gold, that very few depositors ever came back to the goldsmiths except to make more deposits of gold.

41 It soon became apparent to the goldsmiths that since only a small percentage of the depositors ever came back for their gold, the goldsmiths only had to keep enough gold on hand, as a 'reserve,' to satisfy those who did come back.

42 Realizing this, the goldsmiths decided they could safely issue more gold certificates than the amount of gold "on deposit."

43 By this 'fortuitous' (deceitful) circumstance they had discovered how a shrewd unethical goldsmith could issue certificates on gold he didn't have, and become super-rich by "making money out of nothing."

44 What's more, these certificates could be used to buy up all kinds of tangible property; or they could be loaned out to others at interest.

45 Here indeed was the 'royal road' to wealth.

46 THE PROBLEM OF A "RUN ON THE BANK"

47 It was important to keep a good 'reserve' of gold for those who did want to cash in their certificates, but this ordinarily involved only a fraction of the certificates in circulation.

48 Thus "fractional reserve banking" was born.

49 But every once in awhile people would become suspicious that perhaps the goldsmith-banker didn't really have as much gold as he claimed to have.

50 Then there would be a rush (or 'panic') to cash in the certificates to get what gold was available before it was all gone.

51 This is called a "run on the bank."

52 On such occasions the goldsmith-bankers usually tried to allay the fears of those who first demanded their gold, by

promptly hauling out the precious metal and redeeming the certificates.

53 But if the "run" continued they would not be able to keep up their pretense for long, because the bank would run out of gold.

54 When this happened the only alternative was to "close the doors" in disgrace and go out of business, while the depositors paid the high price of the goldsmith's deception and greed.

55 THE CENTRAL BANKS OF EUROPE LEARNED TO AVOID RUNS ON THEIR BANKS

56 As "fractional banking" became an established practice, it did not take long for the wealthy bankers of Europe to realize that if they were to prevent occasional runs on their banks by suspicious depositors who might want their gold on demand, they would have to work out a cooperative agreement with other banking families.

57 It was agreed that if a bank had a "run," all the other banks would quickly pool their gold and send it to the trouble spot until things cooled down.

58 They learned from experience that if a bank could demonstrate that it did have plenty of gold to redeem its certificates, the people would regain confidence in the bank and re-deposit their gold.

59 The yellow metal could then be returned to the various other banks from which it had been hastily gathered.

60 FRACTIONAL BANKERS DO SOMETHING ORDINARY PEOPLE CANNOT DO

61 It is immediately evident that "making money out of nothing" is selling something the money-managers don't really have.

62 It's considered a criminal fraud if a person sells a house he doesn't own. The same thing is true if he sells something which doesn't even exist and never will exist.

63 Then how do the bankers get away with it? The answer is amazing!

64 The bankers saw the danger of their position and decided to protect themselves by getting the government involved.

65 They reasoned that the government wouldn't prosecute the bankers if the government itself

was in on the deal!

66 So this is what the bankers set out to achieve — first in Europe, then more recently in the United States.

67 THE BANK OF ENGLAND

68 In 1694 William III was involved in a war with France. He needed money in large quantities and he needed it quickly.

69 The British coffers were empty so he asked for vast loans of money from a super-rich Englishman, William Paterson, and from some of his wealthy friends.

70 Paterson and his friends were perfectly agreeable to the loan, provided that they were allowed to do two things:

71 (1) Set up a privately-owned bank to be called The Bank of England.

72 (2) receive authority from the King to issue their own bank notes as England's official legal tender.

73 Since "Paterson Bank Notes" would be loaned to the King, so he could build and equip his armies, he readily agreed.

74 This gave legal sanction to a private bank being authorized to print bank notes as the legal tender for the nation.

75 Each bill promised to pay in gold "on demand" but the bankers actually had only a small fraction of the gold needed to cover the vast quantity of bank notes they were printing.

76 By this means the bankers brought the King in on the ruse as a Patron and Beneficiary of a system of "fractional reserve banking" — "making money out of nothing."

77 This gave the King what he needed, and it gave the bankers what they wanted.

78 What did it matter if the bankers were making money out of nothing?

79 King William would have the needed bank notes that merchants would accept as "money" so he could buy the mercenaries and armaments to carry out his war with France.

80 Governments take the same attitude today.

81 The King even went so far as to eliminate any possible competition for the so-called "Bank of England" by giving Paterson and his friends an official Charter from the Crown, and by commanding the Goldsmiths of Lon-

don to discontinue issuing receipts as depositories for precious metals.

82 This drove most of the merchants to store their gold with the Bank of England.

83 So a privately-owned bank became the official depository of the English Crown by printing its own bank notes as the King's legal tender, thereby legalizing its deceitful formula for making money out of nothing, with the government's OK.

84 By any standard, William Paterson considered this fantastic achievement pure genius!

85 It is interesting to note that right at the time William III was setting up this privately-owned Bank of England, based on "fractional reserve banking," the colonists were moving in the opposite direction, developing a system of "sound money" in America.

86 May the grace of our Lord Jesus Christ be with you all. Amen.

CHAPTER 2

BETWEEN 1690 and 1700 Massachusets decided that money should be issued exclusively by the central authority of the government representing the interests of the whole people.

2 At the same time they set out to discover a "natural law" according to "Nature" and "Nature's God" by which they could issue sound and stable money.

3 When money is stable people are encouraged to invest because they know their money will have the same value when they get it back as it had when they loaned it or earned it.

4 Furthermore, stable money encourages people to save because they know it will have the same value when they are old as it had when they put it into savings.

5 Meanwhile, it will have earned a great deal of interest. Sound money is the only way to structure a sound economy.

6 Historically, there are only two ways to make money stable.

7 One way is to relate all currency to precious metals which maintain a reliable degree of stability in their value or buying power.

8 The other way is to maintain the same relative amount of money and credit in operation and only add to the money supply according to the growth of the productivity of the people, the Gross National Product (GNP).

9 Massachusetts issued its own "paper money" and made it full legal tender as of July 2, 1680.

10 This money could be used to pay all debts, public and private.

11 It was used to cover public expenses, finance public works, and was loaned to private citizens for long periods of time at low rates of interest.

12 Notice that these bills of currency were physically loaned out as though they were gold and silver.

13 Furthermore, the treasurer of the colony loaned out currency at a *modest* rate of interest, and the proceeds from this interest were paid into the colony's treasury.

14 This provided public revenue to the colony and greatly eliminated the need for taxes.

15 Meanwhile, the colony paid

no interest for the use of money to anyone.

16 Other colonies began following this same sound procedure, and it soon resulted in a period of unrivaled prosperity for Colonial America.

17 THE BANK OF ENGLAND INVADES ITS AMERICAN COLONIES

18 The greedy owners of the Bank of England decided to harness this prosperity of England's American colonies.

19 The privately-owned Bank of England wanted to force the colonies to borrow "bank notes" from them at interest.

20 Beginning around 1720, the Bank of England induced parliament to suppress all colonial money.

21 Years of colonial defiance began in 1749 when Parliament passed *The Resumption Act,* demanding that all contracts and taxes had to be paid in silver or gold.

22 Gold and silver were so scarce in the colonies that this Act resulted in financial disaster.

23 A deep depression ensued. Prices fell. Trade stagnated. This was the *real* cause of the Revolutionary War for independence.

24 THE EARLY AMERICANS LEARN A BITTER LESSON IN HOW NOT TO ISSUE MONEY

25 Following America's Declaration of Independence, in 1776, the American Congress began issuing their own paper money again, but this time without any limit in quantity — and the States did the same.

26 Since none of this money was tied to precious metal, or limited in quantity, these "Continental dollars" soon inflated out of sight, eventually becoming worthless — "worth less" than a penny.

27 After winning the Revolutionary War, this fatal monetary system almost brought about the destruction of the United States.

28 There was not only skyrocketing inflation, but a deep depression and rioting.

29 The New England States became so antagonistic toward developments that at one point they threatened to secede from the Union.

30 This was the critical situation when the American Constitution was finally conceived to

supposedly save the day.

31 With the adoption of the Constitution, Jefferson hoped the nation would go back to the earlier procedure with government issuing its money based on the growth of the productivity of the people, the Gross National Product (GNP).

32 The treasury could then set up branches for loaning money, as was done prior to 1720 and the Revolutionary War. And all payments of interest would go into the nation's general fund, thereby greatly eliminating the need for taxes.

33 Jefferson's first hopes were thwarted when the gold and silver standard was written into the Constitution (Article I, Section 10).

34 His second hope was shattered when Alexander Hamilton was appointed Secretary of the Treasury, and pushed through a private "central bank" just like the ones in Europe.

35 THE FIRST BANK OF THE UNITED STATES

36 Even though most of the stock in Hamilton's bank was privately owned by many of his associates in New York, it was called "The Bank of the United States."

37 This name led people to assume it was a government bank, but it was not.

38 This same trick was used in 1913 when a group of bankers called their self-styled consortium of financial power the "Federal Reserve System." But we will get to that part of this discussion in later reports.

39 The advantage of the new bank was that it provided immediate credit resources for the nation, which was otherwise bankrupt.

40 This practical reality is what appealed to George Washington, first and foremost.

41 He recognized the dangers involved, but felt these could be circumvented by the fact that the Charter for the bank would end in 20 years.

42 Thomas Jefferson vigorously protested the disadvantages of the central bank, and his dispute with Alexander Hamilton became so heated that finally Jefferson resigned as Secretary of State.

43 Critics of the new bank pointed out that;

45 (1) The issuing of the char-

ter for the bank was without any Constitutional authority, the bank was unconstitutional.

46 (3) It allowed this private central bank to loan out its printed bank notes at interest.

47 (4) This private central bank was made exempt from paying any taxes.

48 (5) It was unconstitutionally designed to collect taxes and serve as the depository of government funds, instead of the U.S. Treasury.

49 (6) The banking act also held the U.S. Government liable for the fiscal transactions of the bank.

50 (7) Only one-fifth of the stock (20%) was owned by the government, so policies and de-cisions-making would always be in the hands of the private banks.

51 Jefferson considered the whole scheme an unconstitutional threat to the basic fabric of the American civilization.

52 He prophesied:

53 *"If the American people allow the banks to control the issuance of their currency, first by inflation and then by deflation, the banks and corporations that will grown up around them will deprive the people of all prop-erty until their children will wake up homeless on the continent that their fathers occupied."*

54 *"The issuing power of money should be taken away from the banks and restored to Congress and to the people to whom it belongs."* (Oliver Cusing Swinell, The Story of Our Money, Forham Publishing Co., Hawthorne, CA., 1964, p.84).

55 THE SECOND BANK OF THE UNITED STATES

56 Dissatisfaction with the first Bank of the United States resulted in its Charter expiring in 1811.

57 Resulting in the War of 1812.

58 The financial pressures of the War of 1812 ended with demands for a second central bank.

59 The second Bank of the United States went into operation in 1816, with the U.S. Government owning only 5% of the stock.

60 The bank fulfilled its basic function during a period of relative prosperity and was popular with may people.

61 However, President Jackson saw this small body of powerful bankers gradually building a financial kingdom at the expense

of the American people, so he vetoed the act which would have extended the life of the second private central bank.

62 The stockholders of the private bank never forgave him for that.

63 Even so, the policies of Andrew Jackson resulted in the Government getting completely our of debt.

64 He even ended up with a surplus of $35,000,000.

65 He made $28,000,000 available to the various States as "loans."

66 There had never been anything like it before — and certainly nothing like it since.

67 THE BANKER'S FEUD WITH ABRAHAM LINCOLN

68 When the Civil War (*the War between the States*) broke out, the new President found the treasury empty, and payments in gold had been of necessity suspended.

69 Since supplies were desperately needed to mobilize and equip the Union Army, Lincoln appealed to the banks for loans.

70 At that time, there were 1,600 banks chartered by 29 different States, issuing 7,000 different kinds of bank notes.

71 To the Lincoln's shocked amazement these banks demanded 28% yearly interest for any loans granted to the Federal Government in this hour of crisis.

72 President Lincoln immediately persuaded Congress to let him borrow from the American taxpayers without interest.

73 This was done by having Congress authorize the issuing of Government Notes called "Greebacks," promising to pay "on demand" the amount shown on the face of the notes.

74 These notes were not issued as "dollars" but as "promissory notes" authorized under the borrowing power of the Constitution.

75 As the notes were gradually turned in for payment of taxes, it allowed the government to pay off these notes in an orderly way, without interest.

76 Without doubt, these notes helped Lincoln fight the war.

77 Lincoln wrote: *"...we finally accomplished it and gave to the people of this Great Republic the greatest blessing they ever had — their own paper to pay*

their own debts." (Dwinell, The Story of Our Money, p.115).

78 But the banks retaliated, and open hostilities were launched against Lincoln's Greenbacks, and Lincoln himself.

79 By a variety of devious techniques, they induced Congress to pass several bills which seriously distorted everything President Lincoln was trying to accomplish.

80 Circumstances finally forced Lincoln to issue bonds which the banks could buy with depreciated Greenbacks, and then charge the Government substantial interest rates on the depreciated bonds.

81 Even the Secretary of the Treasury joined the Bankers in their demand that the power to issue the nation's money be returned to them.

82 In 1863, Congress capitulated under the pressure of Wall Street and authorized the setting up of a privately-owned system of National Banks.

83 Each bank was given virtually tax-free status and was allowed to print money instead of the United States.

84 By 1839 there were more than 14,000 privately owned so-called "National Banks."

85 After the end of the Civil War, and Lincoln's assassination, the major banking interests jockeyed the economy back and forth in an series of booms and busts that finally set the stage for the biggest coup of all, the creation of the Federal Reserve System (the FED) in 1913.

86 The circumstances which created the climate for the U.S. adoption of an European-type central bank, in the guise of the Federal Reserve system, evolved in an atmosphere of intrigue, political manipulation, and another deliberately fabricated "economic crisis."

87 It would be virtually impossible to believe the crass unfolding of events unless the size of the prize and the avarice of the money-power to capture it are allowed to account for the ruthless tactics that were employed.

88 The record shows that there is certainly **no** honor among thieves.

89 One of the most shocking aspects of the nation's financial history during this period was the savage and unrelenting malevo-

lence with which the top money-managers "cannibalized" each other.

90 In Western vernacular, it was the jungle-law of "dog-eat-dog" or "man-eat-man."

91 What's more, the record shows that when it came to abusing, deceiving, and exploiting the common people, the same jungle code applied, except that the people were far more helpless. They didn't really understand what was happening to them.

92 But in the circles of high finance, all the contestants who were vying for power knew exactly what was going on, and what they were doing.

93 Carefully, stealthily, and viciously they maneuvered their way through the maze of the money markets, seeking to squirm into some surprise position of superior advantage where they could shoot down one or more of their opponents.

94 This was the game the money managers were playing when they intentionally triggered the crash of 1907-1908!

95 May the grace of our Lord Jesus Christ be with you all. Amen.

CHAPTER 3

WALL STREET goes for broke in 1907.

2 The war that took place on Wall Street, which spread economic devastation across the nation during 1907-08, was the direct result of one huge money trust trying to cannibalize its competition.

3 The record shows that the Rockefeller interests of Amalgamated Copper set out to destroy the Heinze combination that owned Union Copper Company.

4 By cleverly manipulating the stock market, the Rockefeller faction drove down Heinze stock in Union Copper from $60 to $10 per share.

5 The rumor was then spread that not only Heinze Copper but also the Heinze Banks were folding under Rockefeller pressure.

6 J.P. Morgan joined in to announce that he thought the Knickerbocker Trust Company would be the first Heinze Bank to go broke.

7 That was all it took to send depositors storming to the tellers of the Knickerbocker Bank to get their money on deposit there.

8 Within a few days the bank was forced to close its doors.

9 Similar fear spread to other Heinze Banks and then to the whole banking world. The crash was on.

10 Millions of people were sold out and rendered homeless.

11 The destitute and hungry shifted for themselves as best they could.

12 Circulating money was hoarded by anyone who happened to have any, or get some, and before long a viable medium of exchange became practically nonexistent.

13 Many business concerns began printing IOU's on small pieces of paper and exchanging these for raw materials, as well as giving them to their workers for wages.

14 These "tokens" were passed around as a temporary medium of exchange.

15 At this critical juncture, J.P. Morgan came to the "rescue."

16 He offered to salvage the last Heinze Bank — Trust Company of America — if it would turn over to him, for a mere pittance of its true worth, the fabu-

lously valuable Tennessee Coal and Iron Company in Birmingham, Alabama.

17 Morgan wished to add this to the U.S. Steel Company which he had purchased from Andrew Carnegie.

18 This arrangement violated the anti-trust laws but in the prevailing climate of crisis the proposed transaction was approved by Washington, D.C.

19 At this point J.P. Morgan told his partners he was intrigued by the "tokens" of paper (the printed IOU's) which various business houses were being allowed to circulate as a medium of exchange.

20 He sold the government on the idea of letting him put out 200 million dollars in such "tokens," issued by one of the Morgan establishments.

21 He said this flow of "Morgan Certificates" might get the economy going again.

22 Government approval was granted and as these new forms of "Morgan Money" began circulating, the public regained its confidence, so that hoarded money began to circulate again.

23 Morgan never forgot how exciting it was to circulate 200 million dollars in "certificates" created out of nothing more than his own "corporate credit" (his name) and the formal approval of Washington, D.C.

24 Here was the super device to make millions!

25 In Morgan's mind, the seeds for the Federal Reserve System had been sown and began to sprout.

26 *It is not always by armies and guns that a nation is overthrown!*

27 HOW J.P. MORGAN BECAME ATTRACTED TO PHILOSOPHER WOODROW WILSON

28 On the surface J.P. Morgan seemed to have saved the day — like crassly throwing a child into the river and then being lionized for afterwards saving him.

29 No one was more fascinated with the new heroic image of Mr. Morgan than Woodrow Wilson.

30 In the early 1900s Woodrow Wilson had gained a tremendous reputation as a writer and educator.

31 People listened to him. He had practically "founded" the Department of Political Science

at Princeton University.

32 In fact, his philosophy of political science permeated universities all across the nation, and to a large extent still represents the prevalent viewpoint today.

33 Wilson reflected a strong criticism of what he called the "archaic nature of the American system of government" and the necessity of getting stronger administrative control over the affairs of the people.

34 In many points Wilson was very critical of the Founders' well thought out constitutional concepts.

35 Wilson wrote: *"All this trouble (the 1907 depression) could be averted if we appoint a committee of six or seven public-spirited men like J.P. Morgan to handle the affairs of our country."* (H.A. Kenan, "The Federal Reserve Bank," p.103).

36 Although reputed to be a great spokesman for "democracy," Wilson actually had a powerful instinct for the further strengthening of centralized power.

37 Morgan liked what Wilson was saying.

38 Soon after Wilson became President of Princeton University, certain Morgan interests began encouraging him to enter the political arena.

39 By 1910, he won the election for Governor of New Jersey; and in 1912, Wilson won the election for the Presidency of the United States.

40 THE DEMAND FOR MONEY REFORM

41 By 1908 J.P. Morgan was already working, through his wealthy friend, Senator Nelson Aldrich of Rhode Island, to establish a private central banking system similar to those operating in Europe.

42 Mr. Morgan could not forget the exhilarating satisfaction of printing and circulating millions of dollars worth of 'certificates' merely on his "corporate credit."

43 This to him was even better than the schemes of the goldsmith-bankers!

44 Meanwhile, public pressure was making increased demands for a plan to eliminate Wall Street control and exploitation of the economy.

45 Accordingly, Morgan's friend, Senator Nelson Aldrich,

had been made the Chairman of the National Monetary Commission. Congress assigned this Commission the task of studying the United States monetary system and making recommendations of ways to improve it.

46 The Commission promptly took off for Europe, and after spending $300,000.00 returned to write 20 massive volumes extolling the advantages of Europe's central banking system.

47 This report was barely published when there arrived on the scene Paul Warburg, whose brother Max Warburg, was in charge of the Reichsbank — the privately-owned central bank of Germany.

48 Paul Warburg came well-financed by the Rothschild family who bought him a partnership in the Rothschild-dominated firm of Kuhn, Loeb and Company.

49 Paul Warburg immediately became associated with other Wall Street financial leaders and Senator Nelson Aldrich as well.

50 He then began traveling all over the country lecturing to universities and business organizations.

51 He emphasized the absolute necessity of setting up a new "national" banking system that would prevent Wall Street from putting the nation through those devastating "boom and bust cycles" of the past.

52 He promised that the new system would really "clip the wings" of the big bankers.

53 It was exactly the sound of monetary music the people had been waiting to hear!

54 Little did people know that Wall Street was preparing its own plan.

55 THE SECRET MEETING AT JEKYLL ISLAND, GEORGIA.

56 On November 22, 1910, a private railroad car pulled out of the station at Hoboken, New Jersey, with some notable financiers aboard.

57 Others joined them later.

58 They met at the lavish J.P. Morgan estate on Jekyll's Island, Georgia.

59 This secret meeting included Senator Nelson Aldrich; the professional economist and Assistant Secretary of the Treasury who had traveled with him to Europe; the President of the National Bank of New York; a se-

nior partner of the J.P. Morgan Company; the President of Morgan's First National Bank of New York; Paul Warburg, of the banking house of Kuhn, Loeb Company in New York; and lastly, Benjamin Strong of J.P. Morgan's central office in New York City.

60 By the end of ten days, they had prepared a bill for Congress which was later submitted as the "Aldrich Plan."

61 Five million dollars were pressured out of major banks to "educate" Congress and the American people to accept this plan.

62 The main resistance to the Aldrich Plan came from the House of Representatives where an official investigation had revealed some of the ruthless operations of powerful financial interests on Wall Street, and definitely fixed responsibility on Wall Street — especially Rockefeller and Morgan — for the crash of 1907.

63 With the tide of opposition rising, it was obvious that the Republicans were not going to be able to get the Aldrich plan adopted.

64 Strategy then switched to the Democratic Party which immediately came up with an "alternate plan" to be called the "Federal Reserve System."

65 This plan was almost identical to the Aldrich Plan, but with a different name.

66 THE ELECTION OF PRESIDENT WILSON

67 The next task was to defeat the Republican President, William Howard Taft, in the 1912 election, and to install a Democratic administration in power.

68 Taft was popular but opposed to the Aldrich Plan.

69 It was therefore decided to have another Republican, Teddy Roosevelt, run on an independent ticket to split the Republican vote.

70 The Morgan officials who managed Teddy Roosevelt's campaign were later found to have also put large sums of money behind Wilson as well.

71 As expected, the strategy worked and Wilson was elected President.

THE WILSON ADMINISTRATION BEGINS RESHAPING AMERICA

72 When Woodrow Wilson took

over the White House in 1913, he brought with him his Wall Street advisors, including Colonel Edward Mandell House, who became the major policy-maker and manager of the entire Wilson administration.

73 In his personal writings, House describes the pile-driver tactics that were used to force a bill through Congress that would authorize the establishment of the new Federal Reserve System as a privately-owned central bank.

74 A strong element of deception surrounded the team involved in promoting this legislation; it was "The Aldrich Bill", in new dress, that Congress had already rejected.

75 Secondly, the leading financiers of Wall Street went into a carefully orchestrated act.

76 They pretended to strongly protest against the bill.

77 It was in this illusionary climate of Wall Street antagonism that Congress finally bit the bullet and took a chance on this new wonder-plan which promised to prevent depressions, stabilize the nation's money system and get Wall Street off the back of the people.

78 On December 22, 1913 — three days before Christmas — with that holiday pressuring Congress into final action before the session closed — the House voted that evening 298 to 60 in favor of the new Federal Reserve System (*New York Times, pp.1-3, Dec. 23, 1913*).

79 The Senate began debate at 10 a.m. the following day, and passed what was then called "The Currency Bill," #43-25, at 2:30 that afternoon.

80 There were 48 states, or 96 Senators in 1913, so 48 votes plus a tie-braking vote of vice President Thomas Marshall would have been sufficient to approve the bill even if the 28 absent votes who had left Washington for the holiday had all been cast against the bill.

81 Even so, many of the missing Senators had recorded their positions beforehand in the Congressional record (*Congressional Record, 63rd Congress, 2nd Session, Dec. 23, 1913, pp.1487-1488*).

82 According to the New York Times, President Wilson signed the so-called "federal bank" into law in an "enthusiastic" public

ceremony within hours of the vote (*ibid pp.1-2, Dec. 24, 1913*).

83 Had Thomas Jefferson, James Madison, or Andrew Jackson been around that day, they would have exploded with indignation.

84 By that action, the financial system of the United States was turned over to the Federal Reserve Board that now administers the American financial system of the United States by the authority of a purely for profit group that is mainly interested in obtaining profits from the use of "OPM" ("Opium," "Other People's Money").

85 In this tragic case, the handful of citizens who understood this manipulation by adverse foreign interests, were intimidated into silence and inaction.

86 Those who were critical of the "FED" were quickly branded as "pariahs" in their own fields of endeavor.

87 Today, the American system of government is almost hopelessly compromised by our politicians' dependence on the Central Bank.

88 Without realizing it, Congress had created a powerful engine of private central banking which was given the power to indulge the bankers' voracious appetite for boom-and-bust economics, confiscatory taxation, smothering the nation with indebtedness and the promotions of war on a world-wide scale.

89 No one dreamed that this great power would be used to confiscate the people's gold, diminish their savings with inflation, erode away the value of insurance policies and fixed incomes, destroy the stability of the dollar, and eventually engulf the nation in a miasma of foreign entanglements that would threaten the very existence of the United States as a free and independent people.

90 An Illuminati Oligarchy now controls the United States Government and oppresses the American people by confiscating more and more of their income (their property) through usury, printing press inflation, and the unconstitutional federal income tax!

91 May the grace of our Lord Jesus Christ be with you all. Amen.

CHAPTER 4

THE American colonists had suffered so much from the interference of the British money-trust and the Bank of England in their economy, that they structured the Constitution so issuing money and fixing its value would be under the exclusive control of the people, through Congress.

2 But unfortunately, their original design was never carried out.

3 From the very beginning the vested interests of the private money trusts usurped control of the country's finances and made fabulous profits by carefully engineering boom and bust cycles, which came on an average of once every seven to fifteen years.

4 As mentioned, one of the worst of these "busts" came in 1907-08, and the outcry from coast-to-coast was "Monetary Reform!"

5 So the Federal Reserve was set up with elaborate controls that promised some very exciting things.

6 Supporters claimed that it would stabilize the dollar, prevent depressions and promote prosperity.

7 The fact that the entire operation would be in direct violation of the Constitution seemed trivial compared to all of the marvelous things it promised to accomplish.

8 HOW AMERICA ADOPTED THE IDEA OF A PRIVATELY-OWNED CENTRAL BANK

9 In spite of the warnings of Jefferson, Jackson, Lincoln, and the provisions of the U.S. Constitution, Wilson ran for President on the platform of adopting a privately-owned central banking system to be called the "Federal Reserve."

10 Wilson promised that the Federal Reserve would get the nation out from under the oppressive control of Wall Street.

11 But the public was never told, however, that The Federal Reserve Act had been written and promoted by the Wall Street money-trust itself!

12 Wilson had come to trust these men. They had financed his campaign for President.

13 But in 1916, just three years after the Federal Reserve System got into operation, President Wilson suddenly realized what a virtually uncontrollable power mo-

nopoly had been vested in the nation's new Federal Reserve System.

14 He wrote: *"A great industrial nation is controlled by its system of credit. Our system of credit is concentrated in the Federal Reserve System.*

15 *"The growth of the nation, therefore, and all our activities are in the hands of but a few men.*

16 *"We have come to be one of the worst ruled, one of the most completely controlled and dominated governments in the civilized world, — no longer a government by free opinion, no longer a government by conviction and majority vote, but a government by the opinion and force of small groups of dominant men."* (Quoted in "National Economy and the Banking System," Senate Documents Co. 3, No. 23, 76th Congress, 1st session, 1939.)

17 Wilson's protest against the "force" of a few dominant men is especially noteworthy in view of the many articles he had written as head of the Political Science Department at Princeton University, criticizing the Found-

ing Fathers, calling for more centralized power in Washington.

18 These men from whom President Wilson was feeling such duress in 1916 were the very ones he had been praising a few years before.

19 By 1916 the superior wisdom of the Founding Fathers had become increasingly apparent.

20 ADDITIONAL MORN-ERS

21 The Federal Reserve Act was sponsored by Senator Robert Owen and Senator Carter Glass. Senator Owen was chairman of the Senate Banking and Currency Committee where the bill was drafted. The original bill required the Federal Reserve to maintain stable money which would produce a stable price level.

22 Very shortly Senator Owen also became one of the mourners and wrote: *"This provision was stricken out in the House under the leadership of Carter Glass. I was unable to keep this mandatory provision in the Bill because of secret hostilities developed against it, that at that time I did not fully understand."*

23 But Owen later found out where these hostilities were

coming from. He said: *"Under the administrations of Wilson, Harding, Coolidge, and Hoover, this Act was diverted from its proper purpose, on the advice of those who controlled the policies of a number of the largest banks."* (Gertrude M. Coogan, "Money Creators," p.ix.)

24 Owen spent the rest of his life trying to get the Federal Reserve System repealed.

25 The Federal Reserve Act never would have passed the House without the support of the Democratic Party whip, William Jennings Bryan, who later became Secretary of State.

26 Bryan also became a mourner and wrote: *"In my long political career, the one thing I genuinely regret is my part in getting the banking and currency legislation enacted into law."* (Quoted by H.S. Kenan, "The Federal Reserve Bank," 1967 ed. rev., p.125.)

27 All of these powerful politicians who had so much to do with adoption of the Federal Reserve System, found that this Goliath was too big and too powerful to control or repeal once it had become entrenched.

28 All they could do was mourn.

29 There are *three things* Jefferson, Jackson and Lincoln identified as outright enemies of a sound money system, and The Federal Reserve involves all three.

30 <u>FIRST</u>: PRIVATE BANKERS SHOULD NEVER PRINT THE CURRENCY OF THE NATION

31 The nation should never turn over to a group of private bankers the right to print the official currency of the nation.

32 This right is inherent in the people and belongs to the people's government.

33 Whenever this right has been delegated to private bankers they have always used it to abuse the people and to gradually devour the wealth of the nation.

34 When Abraham Lincoln was not able to initiate a monetary reform act, but was forced to accept the National Bank Act of 1863, he wrote: *"I see in the near future a crisis approach which unnerves me and causes me to tremble for the safety of my country.*

35 *"Banking corporations*

have been enthroned; an era of corruption in high places will follow and the money powers of the country will prolong its reign by working upon the prejudices of the people until all wealth is amassed in a few hands and the Republic destroyed." (H.S. Kenan, "The Federal Reserve Bank," p.6.)

36 SECOND: THE NATION SHOULD NEVER BORROW MONEY AT INTEREST

37 Nevertheless, in the Federal Reserve System the private banks, which own the stock of the Federal Reserve, charge the United States interest for borrowing their own currency!

38 The Federal Reserve Scheme not only now provides that all U.S. Currency shall be printed up as Federal Reserve Notes, but if the government wants to use these notes, it must borrow them and give the Federal Reserve IOU's [government bonds] on which interest must be paid until the bonds have been redeemed!

39 Well, what did the banks loan to the government in exchange for these bonds? Nothing, absolutely nothing.

40 The banks pay for the printing of their Federal Reserve notes and then loan them to the U.S. Government, but they are not redeemable in gold, silver or anything else of value; they are just paper, backed virtually by nothing.

41 Then why are they able to charge interest when all they are doing is printing up our own Government's currency?

42 Well, in 1913 the Congress GAVE the Federal Reserve the "legal right" to print our money and that "right" is as "good as gold."

43 If we want to use the Fed's money, we have to borrow it and give them Federal IOU's for the amount obtained.

44 And each IOU [Government Bond] is something on which interest must be paid.

45 This whole arrangement is totally irrational!

46 The chairman of the Banking and Currency committee, Congressman Wright Patman, asked Mariner Eccles, Chairman of the Federal Reserve Board:

47 Mr. Patman: *"Mr. Eccles, how did you get the money to buy these two billion dollars of*

government bonds?"

48 Mr. Eccles: *"We created it."*

49 Mr. Patman: *"Out of what?"*

50 Mr. Eccles: *"Out of our right to create credit money."*

51 LINCOLN DENOUNCES THIS SECOND FALLACY IN GOVERNMENT FINANCING

52 Since it is the Government's right to create money in the first place, why should we have to borrow our own money from the Federal Reserve Banks, and GIVE interest-bearing bonds [IOU's] in exchange for this money?

53 Lincoln said: *"Government possessing the power to create and issue currency and credit as money, and enjoying the right to withdraw both currency and credit from circulation by taxation or otherwise, need not and should not borrow capital at interest as the means of financing governmental work and public enterprises.*

54 *"The government should create, issue, and circulate all the currency and credit it needs to satisfy the spending power of the Government and the buying power of consumers. The privilege of creating and issuing*

money is not only the supreme prerogative of Government, but it is Government's greatest creative opportunity." (H.S. Kenan, "Federal Reserve Bank," 1967 ed. rev. pp.187-188.)

55 By creating and issuing its own money, Lincoln said the people could avoid a "national debt economy" that bankers instinctively promote.

56 By creating our own money, *"Taxpayers will be saved immense sums of interest, discounts, and exchanges.*

57 *"The financing of all public enterprises, the maintenance of stable government and ordered progress, and the conduct of the treasury will become matters of practical administration.*

58 *"The people can and will be furnished with a currency as safe as their own government. Money will cease to be master and become the servant of humanity; true Democracy will rise superior to the money power."* (Ibid. p.188.)

59 THIRD: FRACTIONAL RESERVE BANKING MUST NEVER BE ALLOWED

60 Fractional reserve banking was invented in Europe about

400 years ago.

61 This permits a bank to set up a "reserve" to cover any claims which happen to come in, and then go ahead and loan many times more money on credit than the "reserves" of the bank.

62 By this means the bank loans out and charges interest on something it does not have.

63 With everybody else, it is a fraud to loan, rent or sell something which does not exist.

64 Fractional banking in our nation should have been outlawed 200 years ago!

65 One of the most dangerous devices employed by the Federal Reserve under fractional banking, is its power to bounce the level of required reserves up and down so as to govern the money supply and interest rates.

66 THE MAJOR OBSTACLE TO CENTRAL BANKS

67 Several European leaders recognized Abraham Lincoln as the major obstacle to the European central banks that wanted to exploit the resources and wealth of the American people.

68 When Bismarck, the Chancellor of Germany, learned of Lincoln's assassination, he said:

69 *"Lincoln's death is a disaster for Christendom. There was no man in the United States great enough to wear his boots.*

70 *"I fear that foreign bankers with their craftiness and tortuous tricks will now entirely control the exuberant riches of America, and use them to systematically corrupt modern civilization.*

71 *"They will not hesitate to plunge the whole of Christendom into wars and chaos in order that the earth should become their inheritance."* (Gertrude Coogan, op. cit., p.216)

72 From then until now, the little-known history of American finances demonstrates the tragic accuracy of that prediction.

73 Shortly before he was assassinated, Abraham Lincoln wrote a letter to a close friend in Illinois; here is part of what he is reported to have said:

74 *"Yes, we may all congratulate ourselves that [the Civil War] is nearing its close. It has cost a great amount of treasure and of blood.*

75 *"But I see in the near future, a crisis approaching that*

unnerves me and causes me to tremble for the safety of my country.

76 *"As a result of the war, banking corporations have been enthroned and an era of corruption in high places will follow.*

77 *"The money power of the country will endeavor to prolong its reign by working upon the prejudices of the people until all the wealth is aggregated in a few hands, and the Republic is destroyed.*

78 *"I feel at this moment more anxiety for the safety of my country than ever before, even than when in the midst of war. God grant that my suspicions may prove groundless."*

79 Extrapolating from Coughlin's analysis, with its 1930s perspective, we know now that, in the struggle between the two "evil empires" — *International Communism* and *International Corporatism* — the latter appears to have triumphed.

80 The lust for wealth, power, and world conquest is not anything "new" but its current disguise of benevolence, and *"Peace, Peace; when there is no peace"* (*Jer. 6:14*), IS new.

81 Do not be deceived by these *"Wolves in sheep's clothing."* (*Matthew 10:16*).

82 May the grace of our Lord Jesus Christ be with you all. Amen.

CHAPTER 5

THE original promises of the promoters of The Federal Reserve were so glorious that it appeared to be the height of stupidity to turn down such a marvelous opportunity — the Constitution to the contrary, notwithstanding.

2 All the Federal Reserve asked for initially was the privilege of printing the nation's currency and serving as the government's bank.

3 In exchange, these promises were made, but not kept:

4 (1) <u>TO OPERATE UNDER THE CONTROL OF THE PRESIDENT</u>

5 The Federal Reserve promised to operate entirely under the direction and control of the President and his appointees to the Board of Governors.

6 The Fed escaped from this control almost at once; more than 200 amendments were added to the original Act that gradually altered the entire profile of the Act.

7 Even the Secretary of the Treasury and Comptroller of Currency were eliminated from its Board of Governors.

8 Hundreds of times the Fed has defiantly acted against the interests of the American people, making billion-dollar decisions favoring its stockholders.

9 In these cases, the President and Congress were helpless; unable to intervene.

10 The Chairman of the Board, Mariner Eccles, admitted this to the head of the House Banking and Currency Committee, when he was asked if the Federal Reserve had more power than the Congress or the President.

11 Eccles declared, *"In the field of money and credit, YES!"*

12 (2) <u>TO PAY INTEREST FOR THE RIGHT TO PRINT MONEY</u>

13 Section 16 of the Federal Reserve Act provided that the Federal Reserve would pay the Government interest for the privilege of printing Federal Reserve notes as the nation's currency.

14 But the Act left this up to the Board of Governors, who from the beginning elected to pay the government zero interest for this right to manufacture the nation's money.

15 No legal remedy is available.

16 (3) <u>TO PROVIDE FREE</u>
<u>SERVICES</u>

17 The Federal Reserve promised to perform many banking ser

CHAPTER 6

THE Constitution was inaugurated during the depths of a devastating depression.

2 At that particular time (1787) the whole American money system was based on a sick, terribly bloated dollar that developed during the Revolutionary War.

3 George Washington knew that unless some healthy money were immediately introduced into the economic system, the new government would be discredited and find Itself doomed to oblivion.

4 It was a time of extreme desperation.

5 Alexander Hamilton came up with a plan to monetize the nation's huge war debt by issuing bonds and selling them to private banks.

6 He urged the President and Congress to allow these bankers to temporarily (for 20 years) establish a private bank in the name of the United States and be responsible for the issuing of money, controlling the amount, fixing its value, and financing the United States government.

7 It was this last factor which appealed to President Washing-ton.

8 There was, of course, no Constitutional authority to have the Federal Government set up such a bank, but Hamilton persuasively argued a theory of "implied powers" which has seriously damaged the whole concept of "limited" government ever since.

9 Although the argument was sufficiently strong to impress Congress, President Washington was uncomfortable with it.

10 In fact, he was actually contemplating a veto of the Banking Act when Hamilton filled his mind with such glowing promises of stability and prosperity under this "temporary expediency" that Washington finally overrode his professional instincts and signed the bill.

11 Jefferson later accused Hamilton of complicating the whole scheme with such elaborate trappings that it had confused the President.

12 It turned out that Washington's original anxieties concerning the dangers of the bill were fully justified.

13 By 1798 even Hamilton admitted that the whole thing had

been a gross mistake.

14 He wrote a letter to Oliver Wolcott, the Secretary of the Treasury, urging that the United States abandon the plan he had concocted and return to the original idea expressed at the Constitutional Convention.

15 He wrote that the Government should *"raise up a money circulation of its own"* which would require of course that the Government no longer allow this important task of issuing money to be assigned to a private banking system. (Letter dated August 22, 1798, quoted by Gertrude Coogan, "Money Makers," pp.204)

16 PRIVATE MONEY-MANAGERS PROVE DIFFICULT TO DISLODGE

17 Once the vested interests of the powerful and wealthy money-managers had become thoroughly entrenched, it proved more difficult to remove them than Hamilton had realized it would be.

18 As a result, for nearly 200 years mighty voices have been pleading with Americans to demand that Congress return to its Constitutional money system, but always to no avail.

19 These pleas have been coming from men such as Jefferson, Madison, Jackson, Lincoln, Lindbergh, and McFadden.

20 They have been like voices crying in the wilderness.

21 And because their voices go unheeded, a highly vulnerable and easily manipulated sick dollar has been employed ever since, with all of its attendant evils.

22 The ultimate mistake was setting up a privately controlled central bank in 1913 under the pretense that it was a government controlled agency.

23 What it actually did was to give to private money-managers the power to issue money, control the money supply, regulate the interest rate (which controls the "value" of money) and indulge in "fractional reserve" banking wherein these money-managers were permitted to loan the government "at interest" billions they didn't own.

24 THE CHARACTERISTICS OF A SOUND MONEY SYSTEM

25 Here are the most important characteristics of the sound and

honest money system that the Founders had in mind when they wrote the Constitution.

26 (1) Money should be recognized as nothing more than a unit of value designed to facilitate the exchange of goods and services.

27 The right to create such a symbol, therefore, belongs to those who create the goods and services — the people themselves.

28 It is an inherent and inalienable right which they alone can delegate.

29 In the Constitution the right to create the people's money was delegated to Congress.

30 (2) Once the right to create money is delegated to the people's representatives (Congress), it is unlawful for the Congress to give or sell that right to a group of private bankers or "money-managers."

31 (3) It is the responsibility of Congress to create a healthy dollar or unit of value which will maintain the same relative value from generation to generation.

32 (4) It is the responsibility of Congress to set up appropriate mechanisms to monitor the money supply so that it will remain in balance with the amount of goods and services the people produce.

33 As productivity increases, the money supply should be increased, but only to the same extent.

34 Congress has never provided the machinery needed to fix and maintain the value of money by regulating the supply in relation to goods and services.

35 (5) Machinery should also have been provided so that no powerful group of private money manipulators could suddenly drain off large portions of the money supply so as to cause a depression, or could suddenly add to the money supply and thereby create sky-rocketing inflation.

36 Either of these developments violates the responsibility of Congress to "fix" and maintain the "value" of the dollar as provided in the Constitution.

37 (6) It was also the intention of the founders that the issue of the dollar be locked into the gross national product of the people.

38 Although, throughout the his-

tory of modern man, precious metal has always been the "money of last resort", people ordinarily prefer to use paper money because it is much more convenient to handle.

39 Experience has taught us that U.S. Notes should be redeemable at the prevailing market price rather than some arbitrary price fixed by statute.

40 A statutory price allows speculators to play havoc with our currency.

41 (7) When a certain unit of value has been declared the official legal tender, no bank or individual should be allowed to make loans except in terms of monetary assets which are in actual possession or readily available.

42 Fractional banking, loaning, or "credit" backed by merely a fraction of the loan is inherently fraudulent and should be outlawed.

43 THE INHERENT DEFICIENCIES OF THE FEDERAL RESERVE SYSTEM

44 No one should have difficulty recognizing at once why the present American money system has produced such a sick dollar.

45 From our earliest history the Congress has never fulfilled its responsibility to issue our money Constitutionally and "fix the value thereof."

46 The creation of the Federal Reserve System was the most serious mistake of all.

47 During its operation for nearly three-quarters of a century, here is what it has done to the American people:

48 (1) It has allowed a group of private central bankers to issue the people's money and make huge profits loaning it back to the government at interest.

49 (2) It has manipulated the dollar until it has lost more than 90% of its buying power since 1913.

50 (3) It has practiced fractional banking on the people wherein it was able to use a small "reserve" to loan out many more times as much money on its "credit" so as to artificially expand the money supply and bloat the economy.

51 Then it would withdraw this make-believe money supply or credit so as to contract the economy and provide an excuse to foreclose on farms, homes,

factories and savings accounts.

52 By this means the fractional bankers were able to replace their make-believe wealth or "credit" with tangible wealth which would be later sold at a substantial profit.

53 (4) It is now known that the money-managers backing the Federal Reserve System, lobbied legislation through Congress which forced the American people off the gold standard in 1934 and off the silver standard by 1964.

54 They succeeded in having the people's gold confiscated in quantities which would now be worth several hundred billions of dollars.

55 (5) Studies show that the stock of the Federal Reserve System is known to have been controlled to a large extent by private bankers who operate the central banks of Europe, and they have continually manipulated the American economy and its Federal Reserve System to their own selfish advantage.

56 By alternately using war and depressions, they have drained off so many billions of dollars from the American people that it

is now difficult to mentally comprehend the extent of it.

57 Although a few members of Congress tried to expose these frequent manipulations, the intricacies of the Federal Reserve System have been too complex, and most Congressmen fail to realize what is actually happening.

58 (6) Most importantly, the managers back of the Federal Reserve System have accumulated such fabulous wealth that they have been able to buy up the major news media, and make such extensive grants to the foundations and universities that it has been virtually impossible for alarmed Congressmen and economists to broadcast their warning through the educational and communications systems of the nation.

59 This media control has kept the public in almost total ignorance of what has been taking place.

60 It has also prevented the mobilizing of the political forces needed to recapture the monetary system from this gigantic establishment of monopolized power which has a vested interest in hundreds of billions of dollars in

the Federal Reserve System.

61 AMERICANS CAN LIB-ERATE THEMSELVES AND SET UP A CONSTITUTIONAL SYSTEM

62 It has been known for years that there is an escape from the present dilemma if a sufficient number of Congressmen can be induced to consider the source of the problem and the requirements for the solution.

63 THE KEY TO SOLVING THE PROBLEM IS SECTION 31 OF THE FEDERAL RE-SERVE ACT

64 Section 31 of the Federal Reserve Act provides that the government can buy back the stock from the Federal Reserve banks at any time, thereby acquir-ing all of the assets that have been accumulating in the Federal Re-serve System during more than three-quarters of a Century.

65 At least two advantages would immediately result from this action.

66 First of all, the stock of the Federal Reserve banks would cost the Government less than several billion dollars whereas the assets of the Federal Reserve System are now more than sev-eral hundreds of billion dollars.

67 Most of these assets are in U.S. Government bonds.

68 There is also another 100 or so more billion being held in "reserve" for the member banks, and practically all of these as-sets are in U.S. Government bonds.

69 Secondly, the Federal Re-serve system has obtained these billions in bonds without paying anything for them and therefore they can be taken back as part of the assets of the System without any obligation to compensate the stockholders for them.

70 In order to understand how in the past the Federal Reserve has been "buying" U.S. Bonds without paying anything for them, it is only necessary to follow the procedure in one of its pur-chases.

71 This is how the Federal Re-serve does it, for instance: The Federal Reserve applies to the U.S. Treasury for 500 million dollars worth of bonds.

78 The Treasury promptly prints up the bonds [Government IOU's] which require the Ameri-can taxpayers to eventually re-deem them at their face value

plus a regular payment in interest.

79 The Federal Reserve puts the bonds in its "reserve" fund and immediately treats these bonds as an asset. It then writes out a check to the Government based on the credit created by these bonds.

80 In other words, nothing of value is surrendered to the Treasury for these bonds.

81 It is simply a question of writing a check on the "credit" which the bonds themselves created.

82 When the member banks buy U.S. Bonds they follow the same procedure.

83 May the grace of our Lord Jesus Christ be with you all. Amen.

CHAPTER 7

THERE was a time in this country when to ask some one for whom he worked was considered somewhat of an insult, as it implied he was incompetent, incapable of gainful self-employment.

2 But now, property ownership (net wealth) is not the general feature of our society, as it was before the Civil War, and largely remained until the Great Depression.

3 Rather, net debt and complete dependence on a precarious wage or salary at the will of others is the general condition today.

4 Since the exercise of freedom often includes using material objects such as books, food, clothing, shelter, arms, transport, etc., the choice and possession of which requires some wealth, we are forced to admit that the general condition of Americans is one of increasing dependence, and limitations on our freedom.

5 Since the turn of the century, there has occurred throughout the world a major increase in debt and a major decline in the freedom of individuals, and of states,
to conduct their own affairs.

6 To restore a condition of widespread, modest wealth is therefore essential to regaining and preserving our freedom.

7 What is going on in America today?

8 Why are we over our heads in debt? Why can't the politicians bring debt under control? Why are so many people - often both parents now - working at low-paying, dead-end jobs and still making do with less? What is the future of the American economy and way of life today?

9 Why does the government tell us inflation is low, when the buying power of our paychecks is declining at an alarming rate? Only a generation ago, bread was a quarter and you could get a new car for $1,995. !

10 Are we headed into an economic crash of unprecedented proportions - one which will make the crash of 1929 and the Great Depression which followed look like a Sunday school picnic?

11 If so, can we prevent it? Or, will we simply arrive at the same point through more inflation-caused poverty, robbing Ameri-

cans of their savings, fixed incomes and wages by imperceptible degrees - reducing their purchasing power. What can we do to protect our families?

12 Some reliable experts say a crash is coming. They also say that there are simple, inexpensive things anyone can do to protect their families - to keep food on the table and a roof over our heads even in the worst of times.

13 But to do that, we have to understand why a depression is coming, who's behind it, what they want, and how the perpetrators plan on protecting their families. Armed with this knowledge, any of us can ride out the coming storm.

14 Larry Bates was a bank president for eleven years. As a member of the Tennessee House of Representatives, he chaired the committee on Banking and Commerce. He's also a former professor of economics and the author of the best-selling book *The New Economic Disorder.*

15 *"I can tell you right now that there is going to be a crash of unprecedented proportions. A crash like we have never seen before in this country. The*
greatest shock of this decade is that more people are about to loose more money than at any time before in history, but the second greatest shock will be the incredible amount of money a relatively small group of people will make at the same time. You see, in periods of economic upheaval in periods of economic crisis, wealth is not destroyed, it is simply transferred into other hands."

16 Banker and former Presidential candidate Charles Collins is a lawyer, has owned banks, and served as a bank director. He believes we'll never get out of debt because the Federal Reserve is in control of our money.

17 *"Right now, debt is perpetuated by the Federal Reserve making us borrow the money from them, at interest, to pay the interest that's already accumulated. So we can never get out of debt the way we're going now."*

18 Economist Henry Pasquet is a tenured instructor in economics. He agrees that the end is near for the U.S. Economy.

19 *"When you are adding*

roughly a billion dollars a day to the American economy, we just can't go on. We had less than 1- trillion dollars of national debt in 1980, now it's $5-trillion - 5 times greater in 15 years. It just doesn't take a genius to realize that this just can't go on forever."

20 The problem is that we have one of the worst monetary systems ever devised — a central bank that operates independently of our government, — which, with other private banks, creates all of our money with a parallel amount of interest-bearing debt.

21 This is why we can never get out of debt. And this is why a deep depression is a certainty, for most of our citizens, whether caused suddenly in a severe economic crash, or gradually through continued relentless inflation.

22 The Fed is creating it to enrich its private stockholders, just like it deliberately created the Great Depression of the 1930s.

23 The Federal Reserve headquarters is in Washington, D.C.; it sits on a very impressive address right on Constitution Avenue right across from the Lincoln Memorial. But is it "Federal"? Is it really part of the United States government?

24 Well, there is nothing federal about the Federal Reserve, and there are no reserves. The name is a deception created back before the Federal Reserve Act was passed in 1913 to make Americans think that America's new central bank operates in the public interest.

25 The truth is that the Fed is a private (or at best, quasi-public) bank, owned by private National banks (which are the stockholders), and run the Fed for their private profit and gain.

26 *"That's exactly correct, the Fed is privately-owned, for-profit corporation which has no reserves, at least no reserves to back up the Federal Reserve of which are our common currency."* (economist Henry Pasquet).

27 The Federal Reserve Act was railroaded through a carefully prepared Congressional Conference Committee scheduled during unlikely hours of 1:30 a.m. to 4:30 a.m. on Monday, December 22, 1913, when most members were sleeping.

28 20-40 substantial differences in the House and Senate versions were supposedly described, deliberated, debated, reconciled and voted upon in a near miraculous 4-1/2 to 9 minutes per item, at that late hour.

30 As author Anthony C. Sutton noted:

31 *"This miracle of speediness, never equaled before or after in the U.S. Congress, is ominously comparable to the rubber stamp lawmaking of the banana republics."*

32 At 4:30 a.m. a prepared report of this Congressional Committee was handed to the printers.

33 Senator Bristow of Kansas, the Republican leader, stated on the Congressional Record that the Conference Committee had met without notifying them, and that Republicans were not present, and were given no opportunity to either read or sign the Conference Committee report.

34 The Conference Report is normally read on the Senate floor. The Republicans did not even see the report. Some Senators stated on the floor of the Senate that they had no knowledge of the contents of the Bill.

35 At 6:02 p.m., December 23rd, when many members had already left the Capitol for the Christmas holiday, the very same day the Bill was hurried through the House and Senate, President Woodrow Wilson signed the Federal Reserve Act of 1913 into law.

36 The Act transferred control of the money supply of the United States from Congress to a private banking elite; it is not surprising that a bill granting a few national bankers a private money monopoly was passed into law in such a corrupted manner.

36 As author Anthony C. Sutton noted:

38 *"The Federal Reserve System is a legal private monopoly of the money supply operated for the benefit of the few under the guise of protecting and promoting the public intent."*

39 Heroic Nebraska Senator Hitchcock, the only Senate Democrat working against the bill, had proposed numerous amendments to the bill aimed at making the Federal Reserve System a government agency (i.e.

placing control in the Department of the Treasury), rather than a private monopoly, but these were all tabled - so great was the power of the Money Changers over Congress by then.

40 If there is still any doubt whether the Federal Reserve is a part of the U.S. Govemment, check your local telephone book. It's not listed in the blue "government pages." It is correctly listed in the "business" white pages, right next to Federal Express, another private company.

41 But more directly, U.S. Courts have ruled that the Fed is a special form of private corporation.

42 Let's take a look at the Fed shareholders: according to researcher Eric Samuelson, as of November, 1997, the Federal Reserve Bank of New York (which completely dominates the other eleven branches through stock ownership, control, influence, having the only permanent voting seat on the Federal Open Market Committee and by handling all open market bond transactions), which has 19,752,655 shares outstanding, was majority-owned by two banks - Chase Manhattan bank (now merged with Chemical Bank) with 6,389,445 shares or 32.35%, and Citibank, N.A., with 4,051,851 shares or 20.51%. Together those two banks own 10,441,295 shares or 52.86%: majority control.

43 While majority ownership conclusively demonstrates effective control, it is not critical to control, which is often exercised in large, publicly-traded corporations by blocks of as little as 25%, and even 2% when the other owners hold smaller blocks.

44 Why can't Congress do something about this dangerous concentration of power? Most members of Congress just don't understand the system, and the few who do are afraid to speak up.

45 For example, initially a veteran Congressman asked if he could be interviewed. However, both times when a camera crew arrived at his office to do the interview, the Congressman never appeared, and eventually got cold feet and withdrew his request.

46 Fighting the bankers is a

good way to see one's opponent get heavily funded in the next election.

47 But a few others in Congress have been bolder over the years. Here are three quick examples.

48 In 1923, Representative Charles A. Lindbergh, a Republican from Minnesota, the father of famed aviator, "Lucky" Lindy, put it this way,

49 *"The financial system...has been turned over to the Federal Reserve Board. That board administers the finance system by authority of...a purely profiteering group. The system is private, conducted for the sole purpose of obtaining the greatest possible profits from the use of other people's money."*

50 One of the most outspoken critics in Congress of the Fed was the Chairman of the House Banking and Currency Committee during the Great Depression years, Louis T. McFadden (R-PA). He said in 1932:

51 *"We have in this country one of the most corrupt institutions the world has ever known. I refer to the Federal Reserve Board. This evil institution has impoverished the people of the United States and has practically bankrupted our Government. It has done this through the corrupt practices of the moneyed vultures who control it."*

52 Senator Barry Goldwater was a frequent critic of the Fed:

53 *"Most Americans have no real understanding of the operation of the international moneylenders. The accounts of the Federal Reserve System have never been audited. It operates outside the control of Congress and manipulates the credit of the United States"*

54 Does that power affect you?

55 Larry Bates said this.

56 *"The Fed is more powerful than the federal government. It is more powerful than the President, Congress or the courts. Let me prove my case. The Fed determines what the average person's car payment and house payment are going to be and whether they have a job or not. And I submit to you - that is total control. The Fed is the largest single creditor of the U.S. Government. What does Proverbs tell us? The borrower is servant to the lender."*

57 What one has to understand is that from the day the Constitution was adopted right up to today, the folks who profit from privately owned central banks, like the Fed, or, as President Madison called them, the "Money Changers", have fought a running battle for control over who gets to issue America's money.

58 Why is who issues the money so important? Think of money as just another commodity. If you have a monopoly on a commodity that everyone needs, everyone wants, and nobody has enough of, there are lots of ways to make a profit and also exert tremendous political influence.

59 That's what this battle is all about. Throughout the history of the United States, the money power has gone back and forth between Congress and some sort of privately-owned central bank.

60 The American people fought off four privately-owned central banks, before succumbing to the first stage of a fifth privately-owned central bank during a time of national weakness — the Civil War.

61 The founding fathers knew the evils of a privately-owned central bank. First of all, they had seen how the privately-owned British central bank, the Bank of England, had run up the British national debt to such an extent that Parliament had been forced to place unfair taxes on the American colonies.

62 In fact, as we'll see later, Ben Franklin claimed that this was the real cause of the American Revolution.

63 Most of the founding fathers realized the potential dangers of banking, and feared bankers' accumulation of wealth and power.

64 Jefferson put it this way:

65 *"I sincerely believe that banking institutions are more dangerous to our liberties than standing armies. Already they have raised up a money aristocracy that has set the government at defiance. The issuing power should be taken from the banks and restored to the people to whom it properly belongs."*

66 That succinct statement is in fact, the solution to most of our economic problems today.

67 James Madison, the main author of the Constitution, agreed. Interestingly, he called those behind the central bank scheme

"Money Changers."

68 Madison strongly criticized their actions in these words.

69 *"History records that the Money Changers have used every form of abuse, intrigue, deceit, and violent means possible to maintain their control over governments by controlling money and its issuance."*

70 The battle over who gets to issue our money has been the pivotal issue throughout the history of the United States; wars are fought over it; depressions are caused to acquire it; yet after World War I, this battle was rarely mentioned in newspapers or history books. Why?

71 May the grace of our Lord Jesus Christ be with you all. Amen.

CHAPTER 8

B Y World War I, the Money Changers, with their dominating wealth, had seized control of most of the nation's press.

2 In a 1912 Senate Privileges and Elections Committee hearing, a letter was introduced to the Committee written by Representative Joseph Sibley (PA), a Rockefeller agent in Congress, to John D. Archbold, a Standard Oil employee of Rockefeller's, which read in part:

3 *"An efficient literary bureau is needed, not for a day or a crisis but a permanent healthy control of the Associated Press and kindred avenues. It will cost money but will be cheapest in the end."*

4 John Swinton, the former Chief of Staff of the New York Times, called by his peers "the Dean of his profession", was asked in 1953 to give a toast before the New York Press Club. He responded with the following statement:

5 *"There is no such thing as an independent press in America, if we except that of little country towns. You know this and I know it. Not a man among you dares to utter his honest opinion. Were you to utter it, you know beforehand that it would never appear in print.*

6 *"I am paid one hundred and fifty dollars a week so that I may keep my honest opinion out of the newspaper for which I write. You too are paid similar salaries for similar services. Were I to permit that a single edition of my newspaper contained an honest opinion, my occupation - like Othello's - would be gone in less than twenty-four hours.*

7 *"The man who would be so foolish as to write his honest opinion would soon be on the streets in search of another job. It is the duty of a New York journalist to lie, to distort, to revile, to toady at the feet of Mammon, and to sell his country and his race for his daily bread, or what amounts to the same thing, his salary.*

8 *"We are the tools and the vassals of the rich behind the scenes. We are marionettes. These men pull the strings and we dance. Our time, our talents, our lives, our capacities are all the property of these men - we*

are intellectual prostitutes." (As quoted by T. St. John Gaffney in *Breaking The Silence,* page 4.)

9 That was the U.S. press in 1953. It is the mass media of America today.

10 Press control, and later electronic media control (radio and TV), was seized in carefully planned steps, yielding the present situation in which all major mass media and the critically important major reporting services, which are the source of most news and upon which most news is based, are controlled by the Money Changers.

11 Representative Callaway discussed some of this press control in the Congressional Record, Vol. 54, Feb. 9, 1917, p. 2947:

12 *"In March, 1915, the J.P. Morgan interests, the steel, shipbuilding, and powder interests, and their subsidiary organizations, got together 12 men high up in the newspaper world and employed them to select the most influential newspapers in the United States and sufficient number of them to control generally the policy of the daily press.*

13 *"They found it was only* necessary to purchase the control of 25 of the greatest papers. An agreement was reached; the policy of the papers was bought, to be paid for by the month; an editor was furnished for each paper to properly supervise and edit information regarding the questions of preparedness, militarism, financial policies, and other things of national and international nature considered vital to the interests of the purchasers."*

14 G. Edward Griffin quoting Ferdinand Lundberg adds this detail:

15 *"So far as can be learned, the Rockefellers have given up their old policy of owning newspapers and magazines outright, relying now upon the publications of all camps to serve their best interests in return for the vast volume of petroleum and allied advertising under Rockefeller control.*

16 *"After the J.P. Morgan bloc, the Rockefellers have the most advertising of any group to dispose of. And when advertising alone is not sufficient to insure the fealty of a newspaper, the Rockefeller companies have*

been known to make direct payments in return for a friendly editorial attitude.

17 *"A few years ago, three-quarters of the majority stockholders of ABC, CBS, NBC and CNN were banks, such as Chase Manhattan Corp., Citibank, Morgan Guaranty Trust and Bank of America; ten such corporations controlled 59 magazines (including Time and Newsweek), 58 newspapers (including the New York Times, the Washington Post, the Wall Street Journal), and various motion picture companies, giving the major Wall Street banks virtually total ownership of the mass media, with few exceptions."* (such as the Disney Company's purchase of ABC).

18 Only 50 cities in America now have more than one daily paper, and they are owned by the same group; only about 25% of the nation's 1,500 daily papers are independently owned. This concentration has been rapidly accelerating in recent years and ownership is nearly monolithic now, reflecting the identical control described above.

19 Of course, much care is taken to fool the public with the appearance of competition by maintaining different corporate logos, anchor persons and other trivia, projecting a sense of objectivity that belies the uniform underlying bank ownership and editorial control, accounting for the total blackout on news coverage and investigative reporting of banker control of our country.

20 Nevertheless, throughout U.S. history the battle over who gets the power to issue our money has raged. In fact it has changed hands back and forth eight times since 1694, in five transition periods which may aptly be described as "Bank Wars" — or more precisely: Private Central Bank vs. American People Wars, — yet this fact has virtually vanished from public view for over three generations behind a smoke screen emitted by Fed cheerleaders in the media.

21 Until we stop talking about "deficits" and "government spending" and start talking about who creates and controls how much money we have, it's just a shell game — a complete and utter deception.

22 It won't matter if we pass an iron-clad amendment to the Constitution mandating a balanced budget. Our situation is only going to get worse until we root out the cause at its source.

23 Our leaders and politicians, those few who are not part of the problem, need to understand what is happening, and how — as well as what solutions exist. The government must take back the power to issue our money without debt.

24 Issuing our own debt-free money is not a radical solution. It's the same solution proposed at different points in U.S. history by men like Benjamin Franklin, Thomas Jefferson, Andrew Jackson, Martin Van Buren, Abraham Lincoln, William Jennings Bryan, Henry Ford, Thomas Edison, numerous Congressmen and economists.

25 So, to sum the economic problem up: in 1913, Congress delegated to a privately owned central bank, deceptively named the Federal Reserve System, control over the quantity of America's money, virtually all of which is created in parallel with an equivalent quantity of debt.

26 Though the Federal Reserve is now one of the two most powerful central banks in the world, it was not the first. So where did this idea come from? To really understand the magnitude of the problem, we have to travel back to Europe.

27 May the grace of our Lord Jesus Christ be with you all. Amen.

CHAPTER 9

JUST who are these "Money Changers" that James Madison spoke of?

2 The Bible tells us two times that two thousand years ago Jesus Christ drove the Money Changers from the Temple in Jerusalem. This apparently was the only time that Jesus used physical force.

3 What were Money Changers doing in the Temple?

4 When Jews came to Jerusalem to pay their Temple tax, they could only pay it with a special coin, the half shekel of the sanctuary. This was a half-ounce of pure silver, about the size of a quarter.

5 It was the only coin around at that time which was pure silver and of assured weight, without the image of a pagan Emperor. Therefore, to Jews the half-shekel was the coin acceptable to God.

6 But these coins were not plentiful. The Money Changers had cornered the market on them. They then raised the price of them - just like any other monopolized commodity - to whatever the market would bear.

7 In other words, the Money Changers were making exorbitant profits because they held a virtual monopoly on money. The Jews had to pay whatever they demanded.

8 To Jesus, this injustice violated the sanctity of God's house. But the money changing scam did not originate in Jesus' day.

9 Two hundred years before Christ, Rome was having trouble with Money Changers as well.

10 Two early Roman emperors had tried to diminish the power of the Money Changers by reforming usury laws and limiting land ownership to 500 acres. Both emperors were assassinated.

11 In 48 B.C., Julius Caesar took back the power to coin money from the Money Changers and minted coins for the benefit of all.

12 With this new, plentiful supply of money, he built great public works projects.

13 By making money plentiful, Caesar won the love of the common man. But the Money Changers hated him. Many believe this was an important factor in Caesar's assassination.

14 One thing is for sure, with the death of Caesar came the demise of plentiful money in Rome. Taxes

CHAPTER 10

SORROW *is knowledge; they who know the most mourn the deepest o'er the fatal truth, the Tree of Knowledge is not the Tree of Life."* (Lord Byron).

2 The Chinese were the first to use paper money, known as "Flying Money," (a kind of banker's draft) in 618-907 A.D.

3 About 1000 A.D. private Chinese merchants in Sichuan province issued paper money known as Jiao Zi.

4 Due to fraud, the right to issue paper money was taken over by the Song dynasty in 1024, which then issued the first government paper money.

5 About that same time, Money Changers — those who exchange, create and manipulate the quantity of money — were active in medieval England. They were so active that acting together, they could manipulate the English economy. But these were not bankers, per se. The Money Changers, generally, were the goldsmiths.

6 The goldsmiths were the first bankers because they started keeping other people's gold for safekeeping in their safe rooms, or vaults.

7 The first paper money in Western Europe was simply receipts for gold left at the goldsmiths, made from rag paper, as the ditty *"From Rags to Riches"* goes:

8 *"Rags make paper; paper makes money; money makes banks; banks make loans; loans make beggars; beggars make rags."*

9 Paper money caught on because it was more convenient and safer to carry than a lot of heavy gold and silver coins.

10 As a convenience, to avoid an unnecessary trip to the goldsmiths, depositors began endorsing these gold deposit receipts to others, by their signature — their "credit sign".

11 Over time, to simplify the process the receipts were made out "to the bearer", rather than to the individual depositor, making them readily transferable without the need for a signature. This, however, broke the tie to any identifiable deposit of gold.

12 Eventually goldsmiths noticed that only a small fraction of the depositors or bearers ever came in and demanded their gold

at any one time, so goldsmiths started cheating on the system.

13 They began by secretly lending out some of the gold that had been entrusted to them for safekeeping, and keeping the interest earned on this lending.

14 The goldsmiths discovered that they could print more money (i.e. paper gold-deposit certificates) than they had gold on hand, and usually no one would be the wiser.

15 They could loan out this extra "paper money" and collect interest on it as well. This was the birth of fractional reserve lending — loaning out more money than you have on deposit as reserves. Obviously, this was fraud, often specifically outlawed, once understood.

16 The goldsmiths began with relatively modest cheating, loaning out only two or three times in gold deposit certificates than the amount of gold they actually had in their safe rooms, but they soon grew more confident, and greedier, loaning out four, five, even ten times more gold certificates than they had gold on deposit.

17 So, for example, if $1,000 in gold were deposited with them, they could loan out about $10,000 in paper money receipts and charge interest on it, and no one would discover the deception.

18 By this means, goldsmiths gradually accumulated more and more wealth and used this wealth to accumulate more and more gold.

20 Today, this fraudulent practice of loaning out more money than there are reserves is known as fractional reserve banking.

21 In other words, banks have only a small fraction of the reserves on hand needed to honor their obligations.

22 Should all their account holders come in and demand cash, the banks would run out before even three percent have been paid.

23 This is why banks always live in dread fear of "bank runs". To banks, fractional reserve loans, *"...are a bright joy, as brittle as glass, accompanied by the haunting fear of a sudden break."*

24 This is the fundamental cause of the inherent instability in banking, stock markets, and national

economies.

25 The banks in the United States are allowed to loan out at least ten times more money than they actually have.

26 That's why they do so on charging let's say 8% interest; it's not really 8% per year which is their interest income on money the government issues: it's 80%.

27 This is why bank buildings are generally the largest in town. Every bank is a de facto private mint (more than 10,000 in the U.S.) issuing money as loans, at no cost to them, except whatever interest they pay out to depositors.

29 Rather than issue more gold certificates than they have gold, modern bankers simply make more loans than they have currency (cash). They do this by making book entries creating fictitious loans to borrowers, out of thin air (or rather, paper and ink).

30 To give a modern example: A $10,000 bond purchased by the Fed on the open market results in a $10,000 deposit into the bond-seller's bank account.

31 Under a 10% (i.e. fractional) reserve requirement, the bank needs to keep only $1,000 in reserve, and is permitted to lend out the remaining $9,000.

32 This $9,000 is deposited by the borrower in the same bank, which then must keep 10% ($900) reserve, and may lend out the other $8,100. This $8,100 is in turn deposited in the bank, which must keep 10% ($810) in reserve, and then may lend out $7,290, and so on.

33 Carried to the actual limits of the system, the initial $10,000 created by the Fed out of nothing, gives rise (in roughly 20 repeated stages) to an expansion of $90,000 in new loans, in addition to the $10,000 in reserves.

34 In other words, the banking system, collectively, multiplies the $10,000 created by the Fed out of nothing by a factor of 10.

35 Even so, fewer than 1% of the banks create over 75% of this fiat money. In other words, a handful of the largest Wall Street banks create money, as loans, literally by the hundred billion, charging interest on these loans, leaving crumbs for the rest of the banks to create.

36 But because those crumbs represent billions too, the lesser bankers rarely grumble. Rather,

they too support this corrupt system, with rare exceptions.

37 In actual practice, due to numerous exceptions to the 10% reserve requirement, the banking system multiplies the Fed's money creation by several magnitudes more than 10 times (e.g. the Fed requires only 3% reserves on deposits under $50 million, and *no* reserves on Eurodollars and nonpersonal time deposits).

38 Thus the U.S. currency and bank reserve total of roughly $600 billion, supports a total debt structure in the U.S. of over $20 trillion in debt — roughly $80,000 in debt for every American man, woman and child, which includes the national debt, bank debt, credit card debt, home mortgage debt, etc.

39 The Fed created roughly only 3% of this total, private banks created roughly the other 97% (including intra-government debt).

40 All of this could and should have been created by the U.S. government — without the parallel creation of an equivalent quantity of interest-bearing debt, over the years, used to pay for government expenditures, thus reducing taxes accordingly.

41 May the grace of our Lord Jesus Christ be with you all. Amen.

CHAPTER 11

BUT should all interest, and all banking be illegal? **No.**

2 In the Middle Ages, Canon law, the law of the Catholic Church, forbade charging interest on loans. This concept followed the teachings of Aristotle as well as of Saint Thomas Aquinas.

3 They taught that the purpose of money is to serve the members of society as a medium of exchange to facilitate the exchange of goods needed to lead a virtuous life.

4 Interest, in their belief, hinders this purpose by putting an unnecessary and inequitable burden on the use of money. In other words, interest is contrary to reason and justice.

5 Reflecting Church Law in the Middle Ages, all European nations forbade charging interest, except on productive loans (i.e. on loans generating a profit to be shared with the lenders as their "interest", as a partner, or "silent investor at risk", as we would say today), and made charging interest a crime called usury.

6 As commerce grew and therefore opportunities for investment arose in the late Middle Ages, it came to be that to loan money had a cost to the lender in lost gain given up, and in risks. So such "extrinsic" charges were allowed, as was profit-sharing on productive investments, but not interest per se as pure (or "intrinsic") gain from a loan.

7 But all moralists, no matter what religion or what their position on usury, condemn fraud, oppression of the poor and injustice as clearly immoral.

8 As we will see, fractional reserve lending is rooted in fraud, results in widespread poverty, oppression of the poor, and reduces the value of everyone else's money.

9 Ignorance has largely silenced moral condemnation of this technique.

10 Unfortunately, some religious schools limit their condemnation of fraud, oppression and injustice to only that conducted against only their own people.

11 This deplorable limitation, which arises out of an exclusiveness in justice and charity, is one of the causes of this banking problem when other peoples

come to be regarded as inferior or subhuman.

12 This inevitably results in a world view in which "peace" means the predominance of the "superior" peoples of the "superior" race — a gross form of crude materialism which is merely a concealed nationalism, even though it condemns the defensive nationalism it arouses in others.

13 But the principal determinants of nationalism, in its last analysis, are merely psychological and variable, not any inherent "superiority".

14 Men forget that the human species is one great human race with a common origin, a common end, and equality of rational nature, in which there are no special "higher races", as linguistics, genetics, anthropology and other sciences increasingly affirm.

15 Even if there were superior races, surely they should be measured by excellence in virtue, not in cunning and deceit. The differences in peoples should serve to enrich and embellish the human race by the sharing of their own peculiar God bestowed gifts

and by the reciprocal interchange of goods.

16 To return to the goldsmiths: they also discovered that extra profits could be made by "rowing" the economy between easy money and tight money.

17 When they made money easier to borrow, then the amount of money in circulation expanded; money was plentiful; people took out more loans to expand their businesses.

18 But then the goldsmiths would tighten the money supply; they would make loans more difficult to obtain.

19 What would happen? Just what happens today. A certain percentage of the people could not repay their prior loans, and could not obtain new loans on which to repay the old. Therefore they went bankrupt, and had to sell their assets at auction or to the goldsmiths for pennies on the dollar.

20 The same thing is going on today, but today we call this rowing of the economy, up and down, the "Business Cycle," or more recently in the stock markets, "stock market corrections".

CHAPTER 12

KING Henry I — the son of William the Conqueror — ascended the English throne in 1100 A.D.

2 At that time, long before the invention of the printing press, taxes were generally paid in kind — i.e. in goods, based on the productive capacity of the land under the care of the tax-paying serf or lesser noble.

3 To record production, medieval European scribes used a crude accounting device — notches on sticks or "tallies" (from the Latin "talea" meaning "twig" "stake"). Tally sticks worked better than faulty memory or notches on barn doors, as were sometimes used.

4 To prevent alteration or counterfeiting, the sticks were cut in half lengthwise, leaving half of the notches on each piece, one of which was given to the taxpayer, which could be compared for accuracy by reuniting the pieces. Henry adopted this method of tax record keeping in England.

5 Over time, the role of tally sticks evolved and expanded. By the time of Henry II taxes were paid two times a year. The first payment, made at Eastertime, was evidenced by giving the taxpayer a tally stick notched to indicate partial payment received, with the same lengthwise split to record, for both parties, the payment made. These were presented at Michaelmas with the balance of taxes then due.

6 It takes only a little imagination to arrive at the next step: tallies were issued by the government in advance of taxes being paid in order to raise funds in emergencies or financial straits.

7 The recipients would accept such tallies for goods sold at a profit or for coin, at a discount, and then would use them later, at Easter or Michaelmas, for the payment of the taxes. Thus, tallies took on some of the same functions as coin — they served as money for the payment of taxes.

8 After 1694 the government issued paper "tallies" as paper evidence of debt (i.e. advance government borrowing) in anticipation of the collection of future taxes.

9 Paper could be made easily negotiable, which made them the

full equivalent of the paper bank note money issued by the Bank of England beginning in 1694.

10 By 1697 tallies, bank notes and bank bills all began to circulate freely as interchangeable forms of money.

11 Wooden stick tallies continued to be used until 1826. Doubtless, ways were found to make them circulate at discounts too, like the paper tallies.

12 One particular Tally Stick was quite valuable. It represented £25,000. One of the original stockholders in the Bank of England purchased his original shares with such a stick. In other words, he bought shares in the world's richest and most powerful corporation, with a stick of wood as money.

13 It's ironic that after its formation in 1694, the Bank of England attacked the Tally Stick system because it was money issued outside of the Money Changers' control.

14 Why would people accept sticks of wood for money? That's a great question. Throughout history, people have traded anything they thought had value and used that for money. You see, money is only what people agree on to use as money. What's our paper money today? It's really just paper and ink.

15 But here's the trick: King Henry ordered that Tally Sticks be used to evidence tax payments received by the government. This created a demand for tallies and eventually made them circulate and be accepted as money. And they worked well. No other money worked for so long in the British Empire.

16 In the 1500's, King Henry VIII relaxed the laws concerning usury, and the Money Changers wasted no time reasserting themselves; making their gold and silver money plentiful for several decades.

17 But when Queen Mary took the throne and tightened the usury laws again, the Money Changers renewed their hoarding of gold and silver coin, forcing the economy to plummet.

18 When Mary's half-sister, Queen Elizabeth I, took the throne, she was determined to regain control over English money. She issued gold and silver coins from the public treasury, thus taking the control over

the money supply away from the Money Changers.

19 Although control over money was not the only cause of the English Revolution in 1642 — religious differences fueled the conflict — money policy played a major role.

20 Financed by the Money Changers, Oliver Cromwell finally overthrew King Charles, purged Parliament, and put him to death.

21 The Money Changers were at once allowed to consolidate their financial power, and for the next fifty years the Money Changers plunged Great Britain into a series of costly wars.

22 They took over a one-square-mile of property in the center of London, known as "The City of London". This semi-sovereign area today is still one of the two predominant financial centers of the world (with Wall Street). It is not under the jurisdiction of the London police, but has its own private police force of 2,000 men.

23 Conflicts with the Stuart kings led the Money Changers in England to combine with those in the Netherlands, which already had a central bank established by the Money Changers in Amsterdam in 1609, to finance the invasion of William of Orange, who overthrew the legitimate Stuarts in 1688.

24 England was to trade masters — unpopular King James II, for a hidden cabal of Money Changers pulling the strings of their usurper, King William III ("King Billy"), from behind the scenes.

25 This symbiotic relationship between the Money Changers and the higher British aristocracy continues to this day.

26 The Monarch has no real power, but serves as a useful shield for the Money Changers who rule "The City of London" (The City), dominated by the banking House of Rothschild:

27 *"In theory still a real monarch, although in reality only a convenient puppet, to be used by the cabinet* (The City, often called The Crown) *at pleasure to suit their own ends; not able even to exercise the power of pardon that is a prerogative of a governor of an American state and of the President of the United States."*

28 In 1934, (June 20), the New Britain Magazine of London cited a devastating assertion by former British Prime Minister David Lloyd George that:

29 *"Britain is the slave of an international financial bloc."*

30 It also quoted these words written by Lord Bryce:

31 *"Democracy has no more persistent and insidious foe than the money powers..."* and he pointed out that *"questions regarding the Bank of England, its conduct and its objects, are not allowed by the Speaker"* (of the House of Commons).

32 May the grace of our Lord Jesus Christ be with you all. Amen.

CHAPTER 13

BY the end of the 1600s, England was in financial ruin; fifty years of more or less continuous wars with France, and sometimes with the Netherlands, had exhausted her.

2 Frantic government officials met with the Money Changers to beg for the loans necessary to pursue their political purpose. The price was high — a government-sanctioned, privately-owned central bank which could issue money created out nothing as loans.

3 It was to be the modern world's first privately-owned, national central bank in a powerful country, the Bank of England, though earlier deposit banks had existed in Venice (1361), in Amsterdam (1609), and in Sweden (1661) which issued the first bank notes in Europe that same year: 1661.

4 Although it was deceptively called the Bank of England, to make the general population think it was part of the government, it was not; like any other private corporation, the Bank of England sold shares to shareholders to get started.

5 The investors, whose names were never revealed, were supposed to put up one and a quarter million (British pounds) in gold coin to buy their shares in the Bank. But only £750,000 pounds was ever received.

6 Despite that, the Bank of England was duly chartered in 1694, and started out in the business of loaning out several times the money it supposedly had in reserves, all at interest.

7 In exchange, the new bank would loan British politicians as much as they wanted. The debt was secured by direct taxation of the British people.

8 So, legalization of the Bank of England mounted to nothing less than legalized counterfeiting of a national currency for private gain.

9 Unfortunately, nearly every nation now has a privately controlled central bank, the local Money Changers using the Bank of England as the basic model.

10 Such is the power of these central banks that they soon take total control over a nation's economy.

11 The central bank soon amounts to nothing but a plutoc-

racy ruled by the rich, and the bankers soon come to be the dominant super-rich class in the nation.

12 This is like putting control of the army in the hands of the Mafia. The danger of tyranny is extreme.

13 Yes, we need a central monetary authority — but one owned and controlled by the government, not by bankers for their private profit.

14 Sir William Pitt, speaking to the House of Lords in 1770 stated:

15 *"There is something behind the throne greater than the king himself."*

16 This reference to the Money Changers behind the Bank of England gave birth to the expression *"the power behind the throne."*

17 In 1844, Benjamin Disraeli, in a veiled allusion to this same power wrote:

18 *"The world is governed by very different personages from what is imagined by those who are not behind the scenes."*

19 On November 21, 1933, President Franklin D. Roosevelt, in a letter to a confidant, wrote:

20 *"The real truth of the matter is, as you and I know, that a financial element in the large centers has owned government ever since the days of Andrew Jackson..."*

21 [Note: Besides FDR's main point, this amounts to high praise for President Jackson, as we will see.]

22 The central bank scam is really a hidden tax, but one that benefits private banks more than the government.

23 The government sells bonds to pay for things for which the government does not have the political wisdom or will to raise taxes to pay.

24 But about 10% of the bonds are purchased with money the central bank creates out of nothing. The government then spends this new money.

25 Once deposited, private banks use these new deposits to create ten times as much in new fractional reserve loans. This provides the economy with the additional money needed to purchase the other 90% of the new bonds, without drying up capital markets and forcing up interest rates.

26 By borrowing the money (i.e. selling new bonds), the government spreads the inflationary effects out over the term of the bonds. Thus there is little to no *immediate* inflation.

27 More money in circulation makes your money worth less.

28 The politicians get as much money as they want, and the people pay for it in eventual inflation, which erodes the purchasing power of their savings, fixed incomes and wages.

29 The perverse beauty of the plan is that not one person in a thousand can figure it out because it's deliberately hidden behind complex-sounding economics gibberish. The full effects of the inflation are only experienced much later - too late to stop.

30 With the formation of the Bank of England, the nation was soon awash in money. Prices throughout the country doubled. Massive loans were granted for just about any wild scheme. One venture proposed draining the Red Sea to recover gold supposedly lost when the Egyptian army drowned pursuing Moses and the Israelites.

31 By 1698, just four years later, government debt had grown from the initial 1-1/4 million pounds to 16 million. Naturally, taxes were increased and then increased again to pay for all this.

32 With the British money supply firmly in their grip, the British economy began a wild roller coaster series of booms and depressions exactly the sort of thing a central bank claims it is designed to prevent.

33 As Eddie George, Governor of the Bank of England, stated:

34 *"There are two things which are intrinsic not just to the Bank of England, but to central banking generally. The first is an involvement in the formation of monetary policy with the specific objective of achieving monetary stability."*

35. May the grace of our Lord Jesus Christ be with you all. Amen.

CHAPTER 14

FIFTY years after the Bank of England opened its doors, a goldsmith in Frankfort Germany, named Amschel Moses Bauer, opened a coin shop — a counting house — in 1743.

2 Over the door he placed a sign depicting a Roman Eagle on a Red Shield. The shop became known as the "Red Shield" firm, or in German "Rothschild".

3 When his son, Meyer Amschel Bauer, inherited the business, he decided to change his name to "Rothschild".

4 Meyer Rothschild soon learned that to loan money to governments and kings was more profitable than loaning money to private individuals. Not only were the loans bigger, but they were secured by the nation's taxes.

5 Meyer Rothschild had five sons.

6 He trained them all in the secret techniques of money creation and manipulation, then sent them to the major capitals of Europe to open branch offices of the family banking business.

7 He directed that one son in each generation was to rule the family business; women excluded.

8 His first son, Amschel, stayed in Frankfort to mind the hometown bank. His second son, Solomon was sent to Vienna. His third son, Nathan, clearly the most clever, was sent to London, in 1798, at the age of 21, a hundred years after the founding of the Bank of England. His fourth son, Karl, went to Naples. His fifth son, Jakob (James), went to Paris.

9 *"There is evidence that when the five brothers spread out to the five provinces of the financial empire of Europe, they had some secret help in the accumulation of these enormous sums, that they were the treasurers of this first Comintern, but others say, and I think with better reason, that the Rothschilds were not the treasurers, but the chiefs."* (C.G. Rakovsky).

10 In 1785, Meyer moved his entire family to a larger house, a five story dwelling he shared with the Schiff family.

11 This house was known as the "Green Shield" house. The Rothschilds and the Schiffs would play a central role in the

rest of European financial history, and in that, the United States and the world.

12 The Schiffs' grandson moved to New York and helped fund the Bolshevik coup d'etat in Russia in 1917.

13 The Rothschilds broke into dealings with European royalty in Wilhelmshohe, the palace of the wealthiest man in Germany — in fact, the wealthiest monarch in all of Europe — Prince William of Hesse-Cassel.

14 At first, the Rothschilds were only helping William speculate in precious coins. But when Napoleon chased Prince William into exile, William sent £550,000 (a gigantic sum at that time equivalent to many millions of current U.S. dollars) to Nathan Rothschild in London with instructions from him to buy Consola — British government bonds also called government stock.

15 But Rothschild used the money for his own purposes. With Napoleon on the loose, the opportunities for highly profitable wartime investments were nearly limitless.

16 William returned to Wilhelmshohe, sometime prior to the Battle of Waterloo in 1815. Then he summoned the Rothschilds and demanded his money back.

17 The Rothschilds returned William's money with the 8% interest the British Consols would have paid him had the investment actually been made.

18 But the Rothschilds kept all the vast wartime profits they had made using Wilhelm's money — a shady practice in any century.

19 Partly by such practices, Nathan Rothschild was able to later brag that in the seventeen years he had been in England, he had increased his original £20,000 stake given to him by his father by 2,500 times (= £50,000,000), a truly vast sum, comparable to billions of current U.S. dollars of buying power.

20 As early as 1817, the director of the Prussian Treasury, on a visit to London, wrote that Nathan Rothschild had...

21 *"incredible influence upon all financial affairs here in London. It is widely stated that he entirely regulates the rate of exchange in the City. His power as a banker is enormous."*

22 Austrian Prince Metternich's secretary wrote of the Rothschilds as early as 1818 that...

23 *"they are the richest family in Europe".*

24 By cooperating within the family, using fractional reserve banking techniques, the Rothschilds' banks soon grew unbelievably wealthy. By the mid-1800s, they dominated all European banking, and were certainly the wealthiest family in the world. A large part of the profligate nobility of Europe became deeply indebted to them.

25 In virtue of their presence in five nations as bankers, they were effectively autonomous — an entity independent from the nations in which they operated.

26 If one nation's policies were displeasing to them or their interests, they could simply do no further lending there, or lend to those nations or groups opposed to such policies.

27 Only they knew where their gold and other reserves were located, thus shielding them from government seizure, penalty, pressure or taxation, as well as effectively making any national investigation or audit meaningless.

28 Only they knew the extent (or paucity) of their fractional reserves, scattered in five nations — a tremendous advantage over purely national banks engaging in fractional reserve banking too.

29 It was precisely their international character that gave them unique advantages over national banks and governments, and that was precisely what rulers and national parliaments should have prohibited, but did not.

30 This remains true of international or multi-national banks to this very day, and is the driving force of globalization — the push for one-world government.

31 The Rothschilds provided huge loans to establish monopolies in various industries, thereby guaranteeing the borrowers' ability to repay the loans by raising prices without fear of price competition, while increasing the Rothschild's economic and political power.

32 They financed Cecil Rhodes, making it possible for him to establish a monopoly over the gold fields of South Africa and the deBeers Firm over diamonds. In

America, they financed the monopolization of railroads.

33 The National City Bank of Cleveland, which was identified in Congressional hearings as one of three Rothschild banks in the United States, provided John D. Rockefeller with the money to begin his monopolization of the oil refinery business, resulting in Standard Oil.

34 Jacob Schiff, who had been born into the Rothschild "Green Shield" house in Frankfort and who was then the principal Rothschild agent in the U.S., advised Rockefeller and developed the infamous rebate deal Rocke-feller secretly demanded from railroads shipping his competitors' oil.

35 These same railroads were already monopolized by Rothschild control through agents and allies J.P. Morgan and Kuhn, Loeb & Company (Schiff was on the Board) which together controlled 95% of all U.S. railroad mileage.

36 By 1850, James Rothschild, the heir of the French branch of the family, was said to be worth 600 million French francs — 150 million more than all the other

bankers in France put together.

37 James had been established in Paris in 1812 with a capital of $200,000 by Mayer Amschel. At the time of his death in 1868, 56 years later, his annual income was $40,000,000.

38 No fortune in America at that time equaled even one year's of James' income.

39 Referring to James Rothschild, the poet Heinrich Heine said:

40 *"Money is the god of our times, and Rothschild is his prophet."*

41 James built his fabulous mansion, called Femeres, 19 miles northeast of Paris; Wilhelm I, on first seeing it exclaimed, *"Kings couldn't afford this. It could only belong to a Rothschild."*

42 Another 19 century French commentator put it this way:

43 *"There is but one power in Europe and that is Rothschild."*

44 There is no evidence that their predominant standing in European or world finance has changed, to the contrary, as their wealth has increased they have simply increased their "passion for anonymity"; their vast hold-

ings rarely bear their name.

45 Author Frederic Morton wrote of them that they had *"conquered the world more thoroughly, more cunningly, and much more lastingly than all the Caesars before..."*

46 Now let's take a look at the results the Bank of England produced on the British economy, and how that later was the root cause of the American Revolution.

47 May the grace of our Lord Jesus Christ be with you all. Amen.

CHAPTER 15

BY the mid-1700s, the British Empire was approaching its height of power around the world.

2 Britain had fought four wars in Europe since the creation of its privately-owned central bank, the Bank of England.

3 The cost of these wars had been high. To finance them, the British Parliament, rather than issuing its own debt-free currency, borrowed heavily from the Bank.

4 By the mid-1700s, England's debt had grown to a staggering £140,000,000 — so the British government embarked on a program to raise revenues from its American colonies in order to make interest payments to the Bank.

5 But in America, it was a different story. The scourge of a privately-owned central bank had not yet landed in America, though the Bank of England exerted its baneful influence over the American colonies after 1694.

6 Four years earlier, in 1690 the Massachusetts Bay colony printed its own paper money — the first in America. This was followed in 1703 by South Carolina and then by other colonies.

7 In the mid-1700s, pre-Revolutionary America was still relatively poor.

8 There was a severe shortage of precious metal coins to trade for goods, so the early colonists were increasingly forced to experiment with printing their own home-grown paper money.

9 Some of these experiments were successful; tobacco was used as money in some colonies with success.

10 In 1720 every colonial Royal Governor was instructed to curtail the issue of colonial money. This was largely unsuccessful.

11 In 1742 the British Resumption Act required that taxes and other debts be paid in gold. This caused a depression in the colonies — property was seized on foreclosure by the rich, for one-tenth its value.

12 Benjamin Franklin was a big supporter of the colonies printing their own money.

13 In 1757, Franklin was sent to London to fight for colonial paper money. He ended up staying for the next 18 years — until the start of the American Revolution.

14 During this period, ignoring Parliament, more American colonies began to issue their own money.

15 Called Colonial Scrip, the endeavor was successful, with notable exceptions.

16 It provided a reliable medium of exchange, and it also helped to provide a feeling of unity between the colonies.

17 Remember, most Colonial Scrip was just paper money — debt-free money — printed in the public interest and not really backed by gold or silver coin. It was an artificial currency.

18 Officials of the Bank of England asked Franklin how he would account for the new-found prosperity of the colonies. Without hesitation he replied:

19 *"That is simple. In the colonies we issue our own money in proper proportion to the demands of trade and industry to make the products pass easily from the producers to the consumers. It is called Colonial Scrip.*

20 *"In this manner, creating for ourselves our own paper money, we control its purchasing power, and we pay no inter-*

est to anyone."

21 This was just naive common sense to Franklin, but you can imagine the shock it had at the Bank of England; America had learned the *"secret of money"* and that genie had to be put back in its bottle as soon as possible.

22 As a result, Parliament hurriedly passed the Currency Act of 1764 that prohibited colonial officials from issuing their own money, and ordered them to pay all future taxes in gold or silver coins.

23 This forced the colonies onto a gold and silver standard.

24 This initiated the first intense phase of the first "Central Bank War" in America, which ended in defeat for the Money Changers, beginning with the Declaration of Independence (1776), and ending with the Peace Treaty of Paris (1783).

25 For those who believe that a gold standard is the answer for America's current money problems, look what happened to America after the Currency Act of 1764 was passed.

26 Writing in his autobiography, Franklin said:

"In one year, the conditions

were so reversed that the era of prosperity ended, and a depression set in, to such an extent that the streets of the Colonies were filled with the unemployed."

27 Franklin claims that this was the basic cause for the American Revolution. As Franklin put it in his autobiography:

"The Colonies would gladly have borne the little tax on tea and other matters had it not been that England took away from the Colonies their money, which created unemployment and dissatisfaction."

28 In 1774, Parliament passed the Stamp Act which required that a stamp be placed on every instrument of commerce indicating the payment of a tax in gold, which threatened the colonial paper money again.

29 Less than two weeks later, the Massachusetts Committee of Safety passed a resolution directing the issuance of more colonial currency and honoring the currency of other colonies.

30 On June 10 and June 22, 1775, the "Congress of the Colonies" resolved to issue one million dollars in paper money based on the credit and faith of the "United Colonies".

31 This flew in the face of the Bank of England and Parliament. It constituted an act of defiance, a refusal to accept a monetary system unjust to the people of the colonies.

32 *"Thus the* <u>bills of credit</u> (paper money) *which historians with ignorance or prejudice have belittled as instruments of reckless financial policy, were really the standards of the Revolution. They were more than this: they were the Revolution itself."* (historian, Alexander Del Mar).

33 By the time the first shots were fired in Concord and Lexington, Massachusetts on April 19, 1775, the colonies had been drained of gold and silver coin by British taxation. As result, the Continental government had no choice but to print its own paper money to finance the war.

34 At the start of the Revolution, the colonial U.S. money supply stood at $12 million. By the end of the war, it was nearly $500 million — mainly a result of massive British counterfeiting. As a result, the currency was virtually worthless; shoes sold for

$5,000. a pair.

35 George Washington lamented:

36 *"A wagon load of money will scarcely purchase a wagon of provisions."*

37 Colonial scrip had worked before because just enough had been issued to facilitate trade — and counterfeiting was minimal.

38 Today, those who support a gold-backed currency point to this period during the Revolution to demonstrate the evils of a fiat currency...

39 ...but remember, the currency had worked so well twenty years earlier during times of peace, that the King of England had Parliament outlaw it. And during the war the British deliberately sought to undermine it by counterfeiting our currency in England and shipping it to the colonies "by the bale".

40 May the grace of our Lord Jesus Christ be with you all. Amen.

CHAPTER 16

TOWARDS the end of the Revolution, the Continental Congress, meeting at Independence Hall in Philadelphia, had grown desperate for money.

2 In 1781, they allowed Robert Morris, their Financial Superintendent, to open a privately-owned central bank in hopes that that would help. Incidentally, Morris was a wealthy man who had grown wealthier during the Revolution by trading in war materials.

3 Called the Bank of North America, the new bank was closely modeled after the Bank of England. It was allowed to practice, or rather it was not prohibited from fractional reserve banking — it could lend out money it didn't have, then charge interest on it.

4 If you or I were to do this, we would be charged with fraud — a felony.

5 Few understood this practice at the time, which was of course, concealed from the public and politicians as much as possible. Further, the bank was given a monopoly on issuing bank notes, acceptable in payment of taxes.

6 The Bank's charter called for private investors to put up $400,000. worth of initial capital. But when Morris was unable to raise the money, he brazenly used his political influence to have gold which had been loaned to America by France deposited in the bank. Morris then loaned this money to himself and his friends to reinvest in shares of the bank.

7 Soon, the dangers became clear.

8 The value of American currency continued to plummet, so four years later the Bank's charter was not renewed in 1785, effectively ending the threat of the Bank's power on the United States. Thus the second American Central Bank War quickly ended in defeat for the Money Changers.

9 The leader of the successful effort to kill the Bank, a patriot named William Findley, of Pennsylvania, explained the problem this way:

10 *"This institution, having no principle but that of avarice, will never be varied in its object ... to encompass all the wealth, power and influence of*

the state."

11 Plutocracy, once established, will corrupt the legislature so that laws will be made in its favor, and the administration of justice, to favor the rich.

12 The men behind the Bank of North America — Robert Morris, Alexander Hamilton, and the Bank's President, Thomas Willing — did not give up.

13 Only six years later, Hamilton (then Secretary of the Treasury) and his mentor Morris, rammed through the new Congress, a new privately-owned central bank called the First Bank of the United States, with Thomas Willing again serving as the Bank's President.

14 The players were the same — only the *name* of the Bank was changed.

15 May the grace of our Lord Jesus Christ be with you all. Amen.

CHAPTER 17

IN 1787, Colonial leaders assembled in Philadelphia to modify the present Articles of Confederation.

2 As we saw earlier, both Thomas Jefferson and James Madison were unalterably opposed to a privately-owned central bank. They had seen the problems caused by the Bank of England. They wanted nothing of it.

3 As Jefferson later put it:

4 *"If the American people ever allow private banks to control the issue of their currency, first by inflation, then by deflation, the banks and the corporations which grow up around them will deprive the people of all property until their children wake up homeless on the continent their fathers conquered."*

5 During the debate over the future monetary system, another one of the founding fathers, Governor Morris, headed the committee that wrote the final draft of the Constitution. Morris knew the motivations of the bankers, well.

6 Along with his old boss, Robert Morris, Governor Morris and Alexander Hamilton had pre-sented the original plan for the Bank of North America to the Continental Congress in the last year of the Revolution, in 1782.

7 In a letter he wrote to James Madison on July 2, 1787, Governor Morris revealed what was actually going on:

8 *"The rich will strive to establish their dominion and enslave the rest. They always did, and they always will. They will have the same effect here as elsewhere if we do not, by the power of government, keep them in their proper spheres."*

9 Despite the defection of Governor Morris from the ranks of the Bank, Hamilton, Robert Morris, Thomas Willing, and their European backers were not about to give up.

10 They convinced the bulk of the delegates to the constitutional convention not to give Congress the power to issue paper money.

11 Most of the delegates were still reeling from the wild inflation of the paper currency during the Revolution. They had forgotten how well Colonial Scrip had worked before the War; but the Bank of England had not. The Money Changers could not stand

to have America printing her own interest free money again.

12 Many believed that the Tenth Amendment — which reserved powers to the states that were not delegated to the federal government, by the Constitution — prohibited the federal government from issuing paper money as unconstitutional.

13 The power to issue paper money was never delegated to the federal government in the Constitution; the Constitution was intentionally silent on this point.

14 The Constitution did however prohibit the individual States from "emitting bills of credit" (paper money).

15 Most of the Framers were led to believe that the Constitution's silence on this point prevented the federal government from authorizing money creation.

16 Indeed, the Convention's Journal for August 16 reads as follows:

17 *"It was moved and seconded to strike out words 'and emit bills of credit,' and the motion passed in the affirmative."*

18 Hamilton and his banker friends used this silence as an opportunity for keeping the government out of paper-money creation — which they planned later to privately monopolize.

19 So both the banker and anti-banking delegates — for opposite reasons but by a margin of four to one — agreed to leave out of the Constitution any federal power for paper money creation.

20 This ambiguity left the way open for the Money Changers to do so — just as they had planned.

21 But paper money was not itself the main issue.

22 Fractional reserve lending was the greater issue because it multiplied by several times any inflation caused by the excessive issuance of paper currency. But this issue was not understood by most of the delegates, whereas the evils of the excessive issuance of paper currency were then known.

23 In their belief that prohibiting paper currency was a good end, the Framers were well advised, because prohibiting *all* paper currency would have severely limited the fractional-reserve banking being then practiced, since the use of checks was

minimal, and would arguably have been prohibited as well.

24 But bank loans created as book entries were not addressed, and therefore were not prohibited.

25 As it happened, the federal and state governments were widely thought to be prohibited from paper money creation, whereas private banks were not — it being argued that this power, by not being specifically prohibited, was reserved to the people, including legal "persons" such as incorporated banks.

26 The contrary argument was that bank corporations were instruments or agencies of the states that incorporated them, and so were therefore prohibited from "emitting bills of credit" — as were the states themselves.

27 This argument was ignored by the bankers, who proceeded to issue paper bank notes based on fractional reserves, and this lost all force once the U.S. Supreme Court ruled that even the federal government could charter a bank — the First Bank of North America — which could issue paper money.

28 In the end, only the states were prohibited from issuing paper money — not the federal government, neither private banks, nor even municipalities, were prohibited from issuing paper money (as happened in about 400 cities during the Great Depression).

29 Another error often misunderstood concerns the authority given to the federal government "to coin money" and "regulate the value thereof."

30 Regulating the value of money — its purchasing power or value relative to other things — has nothing to do with its *quality* or metal content, e.g. so many grains of gold or copper, etc., but only with its *quantity* relative to the money supply.

31 The *quantity* of money in circulation determines its *value;* and never has Congress legislated any total *quantity* of money in America.

32 Legislating the total money supply — including currency, checks and all bank deposits — in fact, regulates the *value* (purchasing power) of each dollar.

33 Legislating *the rate of growth* of the money supply de-

termines its *future value.* Congress has never done either, though it clearly has the constitutional authority to do so.

34 Congress has left this function up to the Fed and the 10,000 plus banks that create our money supply.

35 May the grace of our Lord Jesus Christ be with you all. Amen.

CHAPTER 18

IN 1790, less than three years after the Constitution had been signed, the Money Changers struck again.

2 The newly-appointed, first Secretary of the Treasury, Alexander Hamilton, proposed a bill to the Congress calling for a new privately-owned central bank.

3 Coincidentally, 1780 was the very year that Meyer Rothschild made his pronouncement from his master bank in Frankfort:

4 *"Let me issue and control a nation's money and I care not who writes its laws."*

5 Alexander Hamilton was a pawn of the international bankers. He wanted to create another private central bank, the Bank of the United States, and he did so.

6 He convinced the new President, George Washington, to sign the bill, over Washington's reservations and Thomas Jefferson's and James Madison's opposition.

7 To win George Washington over, Hamilton developed the "implied powers" argument that has been used so often since, to eviscerate the Constitution.

8 Jefferson predicted the dire consequences of opening such a Pandora's box which would allow judges to "imply" whatever they wished.

9 Interestingly, one of Hamilton's first jobs after graduating from law school in 1782 was as an aide to Robert Morris, the head of the Bank of North America.

10 The year before, Hamilton had written Morris a letter, saying: *"A national debt, if it is not excessive, will be to us a national blessing,"* A blessing to whom?

11 After a year of intense debate, Congress passed Hamilton's bank-bill and gave the Bank a 20-year charter, in 1791.

12 The new bank was to be called the Bank of the United States.

13 *"Never was a great historic event followed by a more feeble sequel. A nation arises to claim for itself liberty and sovereignty. It gains both of these by immense sacrifice of blood and treasure. Then, when victory is gained and secure, it hands the nation's credit — that is to say*

a national treasure — over to private individuals, to do with as they please." (historian, Alexander Del Mar).

14 The Bank of the United States was headquartered in Philadelphia.

15 The Bank was given the authority to print currency and make loans based on fractional reserves, even though 80% of its stock would be held by private investors.

16 The other 20% would be purchased by the U.S. Government, but this was not done to give the government a piece of the action, it was to provide the initial capital for the other 80% owners.

17 As with the old Bank of North America, and the Bank of England before that, the stockholders never paid the full amount for their shares.

18 The U.S. government put up the initial $2,000,000 in cash, then the Bank — through the magic of fractional reserve lending — loaned enough money to its charter investors so they could invest the remaining $8,000,000, in capital, needed for this risk-free investment.

19 Like the Bank of England, the name of the Bank of the United States was deliberately chosen to hide the fact that it was privately controlled. And like the Bank of England, the names of the investors in the Bank were never revealed.

20 *"Beneath the surface, the Rothschilds long had a powerful influence in dictating American financial laws. Records show that they were the power in the old Bank of the United States"* (Myers, History of the Great American Fortunes).

21 The Bank was promoted to Congress as a way to bring stability to the banking system and to eliminate inflation. So what then happened? Over the first five years, the U.S. government had borrowed only $8.2 million from the Bank of the United States, but due to borrowing by others in that period prices rose 72%.

22 Jefferson, as the new Secretary of State, watched the borrowing with sadness and frustration, unable to stop it.

23 *"I wish it were possible to obtain a single amendment to our Constitution — taking from*

the federal government the power of borrowing."

24 President Adams denounced the issuance of private bank notes as a fraud upon the public. He was supported in this view by all the conservative opinions of his time.

25 Why continue to farm out to private banks, for free, a prerogative of the government?

26 Millions of Americans feel the same way today. They watch in helpless frustration as the Federal government borrows the American taxpayer into oblivion; borrowing from private banks and the rich, money that the government has the authority and duty to issue itself without debt.

27 So, although it was called the Bank of the United States, it was not the first attempt at a privately-owned central bank in this country.

28 As with the first two, the Bank of England, and the Bank of North America, the government put up the cash to get this private bank going, then the bankers loaned that money to each other to buy the remaining stock in the bank.

29 It was a scam, plain and simple. And they wouldn't be able to get away with it for long; but we must first go back to Europe to see how a single man was able to manipulate the entire British economy by receiving the first news of Napoleon's Waterloo defeat.

30 May the grace of our Lord Jesus Christ be with you all. Amen.

CHAPTER 19

THE Bank of France was organized in 1800 in Paris, just like the Bank of England in London.

2 But Napoleon decided that France had to break free of debt because he never trusted the Bank of France, even after he put some of his own relatives on the governing Board.

3 He knew that when a government is dependent upon bankers for money, the bankers, not the leaders of the government are in control:

4 *"The hand that gives is above the hand that receives. Money has no motherland; financiers are without patriotism and without decency: their sole object is gain."* (Napoleon of France).

5 He saw the dangers, but did not see the proper safeguards, meanwhile back in America unexpected help was about to arrive.

6 In 1800, Thomas Jefferson narrowly defeated John Adams to become the third President of the United States. By 1803, Jefferson and Napoleon had struck a deal.

7 The U.S. would pay Napoleon $3,000,000 in gold for a huge chunk of territory west of the Mississippi River — the Louisiana Purchase.

8 With that three million dollars, Napoleon quickly forged an army and set off across Europe, conquering everything in his path.

9 But England, and the Bank of England, quickly rose to oppose him by financing every nation in his path, reaping the enormous profits of war. Prussia, Austria, and finally Russia all went heavily into debt in a futile attempt to stop Napoleon.

10 Four years later with the main Army of France in Russia, 30-year-old Nathan Rothschild — the head of the London office of the Rothschild family — took charge of a bold plan to smuggle a much-needed shipment of gold, through France, to finance an attack by the Duke of Wellington from Spain.

11 Nathan later bragged at a dinner party in London that it was the best business he ever done. He made money on each step of the shipment.

12 Little did he know that he

would do much better business in the near future.

13 Wellington's attacks from the south, and other defeats, forced Napoleon to abdicate, and Louis XVIII was crowned as King.

14 Napoleon was exiled to Elba, a tiny island off the coast of Italy; exciled supposedly forever from France.

15 While Napoleon was on Elba, temporarily defeated by England with the help of the Rothschilds, America was trying to break free of *its* central bank too.

16 May the grace of our Lord Jesus Christ be with you all. Amen.

CHAPTER 20

IN 1811, a bill was put before Congress to renew the charter of the Bank of the United States.

2 The debate grew very heated and the legislature of both Pennsylvania and Virginia passed resolutions asking Congress to kill the Bank.

3 The press corps of the day attacked the Bank openly, calling it "a great swindle"; a "vulture"; a "viper"; and a "cobra".

4 Oh, to have an independent press once again in America.

5 A Congressman named P.B. Porter attacked the bank from the floor of Congress, prophetically warning that if the bank's charter were renewed, Congress,

6 *"...will have planted in the bosom of this Constitution a viper, which one day or another will sting the liberties of this country to the heart."*

7 Prospects didn't look good for the Bank. Some writers have claimed that Nathan Rothschild warned that the United States would find itself involved in a most disastrous war if the Bank's charter were not renewed.

8 But this warning wasn't enough.

9 When the smoke had cleared, the renewal bill was defeated by a single vote in the House, and was deadlocked in the Senate.

10 By now, America's fourth President, James Madison, was in the White House. Remember, Madison was a staunch opponent of the Bank.

11 Madison's Vice President, George Clinton, broke a tie in the Senate and sent the Bank, the *second* privately-owned central bank based in America, into oblivion. Thus, the third American Central Bank War, lasting twenty years, ended in defeat for the Money Changers.

12 Within 5 months, as Rothschild was said to have predicated, England attacked the U.S. — and the War of 1812 began.

13 The British were fighting Napoleon, and their war with America ended in 1814.

14 The Treasury printed interest-free paper money to fund the war, but this was not done again until the Civil War.

15 Though the Money Changers were temporarily down, they were far from out. It would take them only another two years to

bring a fourth private central bank back — bigger and stronger than before.

16 May the grace of our Lord Jesus Christ be with you all. Amen.

CHAPTER 21

LET'S turn, for a moment, to an episode that demonstrates the cunning of the Rothschild family, in gaining control of the British stock market after Napoleon's Waterloo.

2 In 1815, Napoleon escaped his exile on Elba and returned to Paris.

3 French troops were sent out to capture him, but such was his charisma, that the soldiers rallied around their former leader and hailed him as their Emperor once again.

4 Napoleon returned to Paris a hero, King Louis fled into exile, and Napoleon again ascended to the French throne — this time without a shot being fired.

5 In March of 1815 Napoleon equipped an army which Britain's Duke of Wellington defeated less than 90 days later at Waterloo. He had borrowed 5 million pounds to rearm, from the Ouvard banking house in Paris.

6 From this point on, it was not unusual for privately-controlled central banks in Europe to finance both sides in a war.

7 Why would a central bank finance both sides in a war? Because war is the biggest debt-generator of them all.

8 A nation will borrow any amount of money for victory. The ultimate looser is loaned just enough to hold out the vain hope of victory, and the ultimate winner is given enough to win. Besides, such loans are usually conditioned upon the guarantee that the victor will honor the debts of the vanquished, therefor, the bankers cannot lose.

9 Waterloo is a battlefield located about 200 miles northeast of Paris, in what is today Belgium. There, Napoleon suffered his final defeat, but not before thousands of French and English men gave their lives on a steamy summer day.

10 On June 18, 1815, 74,000 French troops met 67,000 troops from Britain and other European nations.

11 The outcome was in doubt; had Napoleon attacked a few hours earlier, he would probably have won the battle.

12 But back in London — no matter who won or lost the battle — Nathan Rothschild planned to use the opportunity to try to seize

control of the British stock and bond market.

13 This is the account the Rothschilds hotly dispute:

14 Rothschild stationed a trusted agent, a man named Rothworth, on the north side of the battlefield — close to the English Channel.

15 Once the battle had been decided, Rothworth took off for England. He delivered the news to Nathan Rothschild a full 24 hours before Wellington's own courier arrived.

16 Rothschild hurried to the Stock Market and took up his usual position in front of an ancient pillar.

17 All eyes were on him. The Rothschilds had a legendary communication network. If Wellington had been defeated and Napoleon were loose on the Continent again, Britain's financial situation would become grave indeed.

18 Rothschild stood there motionless, eyes downcast. Then suddenly, he began selling. When other nervous investors saw that Rothschild was selling, it could only mean one thing. Wellington must have been defeated; Napoleon must have won.

19 The market plummeted. Soon, everyone was selling their Consols — British government bonds — and other stocks, and prices quickly fell. Then Rothschild and his financial allies started secretly buying them up through agents.

20 Myths; legends; you say? One hundred years later, the New York Times ran a story which said that Nathan's grandson had attempted to secure a court order to suppress a book covering this stock market story.

21 The Rothschild family sued, claiming that the story was libelous and untrue. But the court denied the Rothschilds' suit and ordered the family to pay all court costs.

22 Some authors claim that the day after the Battle of Waterloo, in a matter of hours, Nathan Roths-child, and allied financial interests, came to dominate not only the bond market, but the Bank of England as well (some Consols were convertible to Bank of England stock).

23 Intermarriage with the Monti-fiores, Cohens and Gold-smiths — banking families estab-

lished in England in the century before the Rothschilds — enhanced the Roths-childs' financial control. This control was further consolidated through the Bank Charter Act of 1844.

24 Whether or not the Rothschild family and their financial allies seized outright control of the Bank of England — the first privately-owned central bank in a major European nation and the wealthiest — one thing is certain, by the mid-1800s, the Rothschilds were the richest family in the world bar none.

25 They dominated the government bond markets and branched into other banks and industrial concerns worldwide. They also dominated a constellation of secondary, lesser families such as the Warburgs and Schiffs, who allied their own vast wealth with that of the Rothschilds'.

26 In fact, the rest of the 19th century was known as the "Age of Rothschild."

27 One author, Ignatius Balla, estimated their personal wealth in 1913 at over two billion dollars. In 1913 the purchasing power of the dollar was more than 1,000% greater than now.

28 Despite this overwhelming wealth, the family has generally cultivated an aura of invisibility. Although the family controls scores of banking, industrial, commercial, mining and tourist corporations, only a handful bear the Rothschild name.

29 By the end of the 19th century, one expert estimated that the Rothschild family controlled half the wealth of the world.

30 Whatever the extent of their vast wealth, it is correct to assume that their percentage of the world's wealth has increased dramatically since then, as power begets power and the appetite therefor.

31 But since the turn of the century, the Rothschilds have carefully cultivated the notion that their power has somehow waned, even as their wealth and that of their financial allies increases, and hence their control of banks, debt-captive corporations, the media, politicians and nations, all through surrogates, agents, nominees and interlocking directorates, obscuring their role.

32 May the grace of our Lord Jesus Christ be with you all.

CHAPTER 22

MEANWHILE, back in Washington, in 1816, just after Waterloo and Rothschilds' alleged takeover of the Bank of England, Congress permitted yet another privately-owned central bank in America — the second Bank of the United States.

2 This new bank's charter was a copy of the previous bank's charter. The U.S. government would own 20% of the shares.

3 Of course, the Federal share was paid by the U.S. Treasury up front.

4 Then, through the magic of fractional reserve lending, it was transformed into loans to private investors who then bought the remaining 80% of the shares. Sound familiar by now?

5 Just as before, the primary stockholders remained secret. But it is known that the largest single block of shares — about one-third of the total — was held by foreigners.

6 As one observer put it:

7 *"It is certainly no exaggeration to say that the second Bank of the United States was rooted as deeply in Britain as it was in America."*

8 So by 1816, some authors claim that the Rothschilds and their allies — some by now related by marriage — had taken control of the Bank of England and backed the new privately-owned second Bank of the United States in America as well.

9 And with Napoleon's defeat, at about this time, they dominated the Bank of France as well.

10 May the grace of our Lord Jesus Christ be with you all. Amen.

CHAPTER 23

AFTER about a decade of monetary manipulations on the part of the second Bank of the United States, the American people, once again, had enough.

2 Opponents of the Bank nominated a famous senator from Tennessee, Andrew Jackson, the hero of the Battle of New Orleans, to run for president. He named his home "The Hermitage".

3 No one gave Jackson a chance at first. The Bank had long-ago learned how the political process could be controlled with money.

4 But to the surprise and dismay of the Money Changers, Jackson was swept into office in 1828.

5 Jackson was determined to kill the Bank at the first opportunity, and wasted no time to trying to do so. But the Bank's 20 year charter didn't come up for renewal until 1836 — the last year of his second term if he could survive that long.

6 During his first term, Jackson contented himself with rooting out the Bank's many minions from government service. He fired 2,000 of the 11,000 employees of the federal government, almost 20%.

7 In 1832, with his re-election approaching, the Bank struck an early blow, hoping Jackson would not want to stir up controversy.

8 It asked Congress to pass a bank charter renewal bill four years early. Congress complied, and sent it to the President for signing. But Jackson weighed in with both feet.

9 Never a coward, "Old Hickory" vetoed the bill. His veto message is one of the great American documents of all time. It clearly lays out the responsibility of the American government towards its citizens — rich and poor.

10 *"It is not our own citizens only who will receive the bounty of our Government. More than eight millions of the stock of this bank are held by foreigners. It is easy to conceive that great evils to our country and its institutions might flow from such a concentration of power in the hands of a few not responsible to the people.*

11 *"Is there no danger to our*

liberty and independence in a bank that in its nature has so little to bind it to our country? Controlling our currency, receiving our public moneys, and holding thousands of our citizens in dependence, would be more formidable and dangerous than a military power of the enemy.

12 *"It is to be regretted that the rich and powerful too often bend the acts of government to their selfish purposes. If government would confine itself to equal protection, and, as Heaven does its rains, shower its favor alike on the high and the low, the rich and the poor, it would be an unqualified blessing.*

13 *"In the act before me there seems to be a wide and unnecessary departure from these just principles. Many of our rich men have not been content with equal protection and equal benefits, but have besought us to make them richer by an act of Congress.*

14 *"If we can not at once, in justice to interests vested under improvident legislation, make our Government what it ought*

to be, we can at least take a stand against all new grants of monopolies and exclusive privileges, against any prostitution of our Government to the advancement of the few at the expense of the many, and in favor of compromise and gradual reform in our code of laws and system of political economy.*

15 *"I have now done my duty to my country. If sustained by my fellow-citizens, I shall be grateful and happy. If not, I shall find in the motives which impel me, ample grounds for contentment and peace.*

16 *"In the difficulties which surround us and the dangers which threaten our institutions there is cause for neither dismay nor alarm.*

17 *"For relief and deliverance let us firmly rely on that kind Providence which I am sure watches with peculiar wisdom over our countrymen. Through His abundant goodness and their patriotic devotion our liberty and Union will be preserved."* (Andrew Jackson).

18 Jackson also declared:

19 *"If Congress has the right to issue paper money, it was*

given to them to be used by themselves, and not to be delegated to individuals or corporations."

20 Later that year, in July 1832, Congress was unable to override Jackson's veto. Now Jackson had to stand for re-election. Jackson took his argument directly to the people.

21 For the first time in U.S. history, a candidate took a presidential campaign on the road. Before then, presidential candidates stayed at home and looked presidential. His campaign slogan was *"Bank and no Jackson; or Jackson and no Bank!"*

22 Incredibly (unless one understands who funds university endowment funds and research dollars) modern historians completely overlook this war between Jackson and the Bank.

23 Yet, his presidency has little meaning without understanding this vital issue.

24 The National Republican Party ran Senator Henry Clay against Jackson, and despite the fact that the Bank poured over $3,000,000 into Clay's campaign, an enormous sum at that time, Jackson was re-elected by

a landslide, in November of 1832.

25 Despite his presidential victory, Jackson knew that the battle had only begun: *"The hydra of corruption is only scotched, not dead,"* said the newly re-elected President.

26 Jackson ordered his new Secretary of the Treasury, Louis McLane, to start removing the government's deposits from the Second Bank of the U.S., and to start placing them in state banks.

27 McLane refused, so Jackson fired him and appointed William J. Duane as the new Secretary of the Treasury.

28 Duane also refused to comply with the President's requests, so Jackson fired him as well, and appointed Roger B. Taney to the office.

29 Taney did as he was told and withdrew government funds from the bank, starting on October 1, 1833.

30 Jackson was jubilant: *"I have it chained. I am ready with screws to draw every tooth and then the stumps."* But the Bank was not through fighting yet.

31 Its head, Nicholas Biddle, used his influence to get the Sen-

ate to reject Taney's nomination. Then, in a rare, public display of arrogance, Biddle threatened to cause a national economic depression if the Bank were not rechartered. He declared war:

32 *"This worthy President thinks that because he has scalped Indians and imprisoned Judges, he is to have his way with the Bank. He is mistaken."*

33 Next, in an unbelievable fit of honesty for a central banker, Biddle admitted that the bank was going to make money scarce in order to force Congress to restore the Bank:

34 *"Nothing but widespread suffering will produce any effect on Congress. Our only safety is in pursuing a steady course of firm [monetary] restriction — and I have no doubt that such a course will ultimately lead to restoration of the currency and the re-charter of the Bank."*

35 What a stunning revelation! Here is the pure truth, revealed with shocking clarity. Biddle intended to use the money contraction power given to the Bank to cause a massive depression until America gave in.

36 Unfortunately, this has hap-pened time and time again throughout U.S. history, though without the blunder of Biddle's arrogant admission, and may be about to happen again in our time.

37 So much for the importance to the common good of central bank independence (or so called "autonomy") from political accountability and control.

38 Nicholas Biddle made good on his threat. The Bank sharply contracted the money supply by calling in old loans and refusing to extend new ones.

39 A financial panic ensued, followed by a deep economic depression. Predictably, Biddle blamed Jackson for the crash, saying that it was caused by the withdrawal of federal funds from the Bank.

40 Unfortunately, his plan worked well. Wages and prices sagged. Unemployment soared along with business bankruptcies. The nation quickly went into an uproar and despair.

41 Newspaper editors blasted Jackson in editorials. After all, he was the President then. The Bank threatened to withhold payments to Congressmen which, at

the time, could legally be made directly to key politicians for their support. Within only months, Congress assembled in what was called the "Panic Session."

42 Six months after he had withdrawn funds from the bank, Jackson was officially censured by a resolution which passed the Senate by a vote of 26 to 20. It was the first time a President had ever been censured by Congress. Jackson lashed out at the Bank.

43 *"You are a den of vipers. I intend to rout you out and by the Eternal God I will rout you out."*

44 America's fate teetered on a knife edge. If Congress could muster enough votes to override Jackson's veto, the Bank would be granted another 20-year monopoly, or more, over America's money — time enough to consolidate its already great power. Biddle's cunning strategy was working.

45 Then something close to a miracle occurred. The Governor of Pennsylvania, where the Second Bank of the United States was headquartered, came out in support of the President and strongly criticized the Bank. On top of that, Biddle had been caught boasting in public about the Bank's plan to crash the economy. Suddenly the tide shifted.

46 In April of 1834, the House of Representatives voted 134 to 82 *against* re-chartering the Bank. This was followed up by an even more lopsided vote to establish a special committee to investigate whether the Bank had caused the crash.

47 When the investigating committee arrived at the Bank's door in Philadelphia, armed with a subpoena to examine the books, Biddle refused to give them up. Nor would he allow any inspection of correspondence with Congressmen relating to their personal loans and advances. Biddle also arrogantly refused to testify before the committee back in Washington.

48 On January 8, 1835, eleven years after taking office, Jackson paid off the final installment on the national debt, which had been necessitated by allowing the banks to issue currency to buy government bonds, rather than simply issuing Treasury notes

without such debt. Jackson was the only President to ever pay off the national debt.

49 A few weeks later, on January 30, 1835, an assassin by the name of Richard Lawrence tried to shoot President Jackson. Both pistols misfired. Lawrence was later found "not guilty" by reason of insanity. After his release, he bragged to friends that powerful people in Europe had put him up to the task and promised to protect him if he were caught.

50 The following year, when its charter ran out, the Second Bank of the United States ceased to function as the nation's central bank.

51 Biddle was later arrested and charged with fraud. He was tried but acquitted, and died shortly thereafter while still tied up in civil suits. The second Bank of the United States went belly up. The fourth American Central Bank War had ended in the fourth defeat for the Money Changers.

52 After his second term as President, Jackson retired to The Hermitage outside Nashville. He is still remembered for his determination to "kill the Bank". In fact, he killed it so well that it

took the Money Changers a full century — until 1935 (with the passage of the National Bank Act of 1935) — to undo the damage and reach the same point in their schemes.

53 Late in life, when asked what his most important accomplishment had been, our war hero Jackson replied. *"I killed the Bank."*

54 Jackson also warned future generations of Americans:

55 *"The bold effort the present bank had made to control the government ... the distress it had wantonly produced ... are but premonitions of the fate that awaits the American people should they be deluded into a perpetuation of this institution or the establishment of another like it."*

56 May the grace of our Lord Jesus Christ be with you all. Amen.

CHAPTER 24

UNFORTUNATELY—even Jackson failed to grasp the entire picture and its root cause.

3 Although Jackson had killed the privately-owned central bank, the most insidious weapon of the Money Changers — fractional reserve banking — remained in use by the numerous state-chartered banks.

4 For example, in Massachusetts by 1862 the state banks had loaned out eight times as much as they had gold and silver on deposit.

5 One state bank had issued $50,000. backed by a total of $86.48. This fueled economic instability in the years before the Civil War, particularly as no reserve ratios were mandated for most of the state banks.

6 Still, the central bankers were out, therefore coordinated monetary manipulation on a national scale was rendered impossible. As a result, America generally thrived as it expanded westward.

7 During this time, the principal Money Changers struggled to regain their lost centralized power and money monopoly, but to no avail.

8 Finally they reverted to the old central banker's formula — finance a war to create debt and dependency.

9 If they couldn't get their central bank any other way, America could be brought to its knees by plunging it into a War, just as they were said to have done in 1812, after the First Bank of the U.S. was not re-chartered.

10 One month after the inauguration of Abraham Lincoln, the first shots of the American Civil War were fired at Fort Sumpter, South Carolina, on April 12, 1861. The fifth and final American Central Bank War was begun.

11 Certainly slavery was one cause for the Civil War, but not the primary cause. Lincoln knew that the economy of the South depended upon slavery and so (before the Civil War) he had no intention of eliminating it.

12 Lincoln had put it this way in his inaugural address only one month earlier:

13 *"I have no purpose, directly or indirectly, to interfere with the institution of slavery in the states where it now exists. I be-*

lieve I have no lawful right to do so, and I have no inclination to do so."

14 Even after the first shots were fired at Fort Sumpter, Lincoln continued to insist that the Civil War was not about the issue of slavery:

15 *"My paramount objective is to save the Union, and it is not either to save or destroy slavery. If I could save the Union without freeing any slave, I would do it."*

16 So what was the Civil War all about? There were many factors at play.

17 Northern industrialists had used protective tariffs to prevent the southern states from buying cheaper European goods. Europe retaliated by stopping cotton imports from the South. The Southern states were in a financial bind. They were forced to pay more for most of the necessities of life, while their income from cotton exports plummeted. The South grew increasingly angry.

18 But there were other factors at work. The Money Changers were still stung by America's release from their control 25 years earlier. Since then, America's

wildcat economy, despite the presence of fractional reserve banking with its attendant booms and busts, had made the nation rich — a bad example for the rest the world.

19 The central bankers now saw an opportunity to use the North/South division to split the rich new nation — to divide and conquer by war.

20 Was this just some sort of wild conspiracy theory? Well, let's look at what a well placed observer of the scene had to say at the time.

21 This was Otto von Bismarck, Chancellor of Germany, the man who united the German states in 1871, a few years later, in 1876, is quoted as saying:

22 *"It is not to be doubted, I know of absolute certainty, that to divide the United States into two federations of equal power was decided long before the Civil War by the high financial powers of Europe. These bankers were afraid that the United States, if they remained as one block and were to develop as one nation, would attain economic and financial independence, which would upset the*

capitalist domination of Europe over the world."

23 Within months after the first shots were fired at Fort Sumpter, the central bankers loaned Napoleon III of France (the nephew of Napoleon of Waterloo) 210 million francs to seize Mexico and station troops along the southern border of the U.S., taking advantage of the Civil War to violate the Monroe Doctrine and return Mexico to colonial rule from Spain.

24 No matter what the outcome of the Civil War, it was hoped that a war-weakened America, heavily indebted to the Money Changers, would open up Central and South America once again to European colonization and domination — the very thing America's Monroe Doctrine had forbade in 1823.

25 At the same time, Great Britain moved 11,000 troops into Canada and positioned them along America's northern border, and the British fleet went on war alert should their quick intervention be called for.

26 Lincoln knew he was in a bind. He agonized over the fate of the Union. There was a lot more to it than just differences between the North and the South. That's why his emphasis was always on "Union" and not merely the defeat of the South. But Lincoln needed money to win.

27 In 1861, Lincoln and his Secretary of the Treasury, Salmon P. Chase, went to New York to apply for the necessary war loans.

28 The Money Changers, anxious to maximize their war profits, offered loans at from 24-36% interest. Lincoln said thanks, but no thanks and returned to Washington.

29 He sent for an old friend, Colonel Dick Taylor of Chicago, and put before him the problem to finance the war. Taylor put it this way:

30 *"Why Lincoln, that is easy; just get Congress to pass a bill authorizing the printing of full legal tender treasury notes... pay your soldiers with them and go ahead and win your war with them also."*

31 When Lincoln asked Taylor if the people of the United States would accept the notes, Taylor said:

32 *"The people or anyone else*

will not have any choice in the matter if you make them full legal tender. They will have the full sanction of the government and be just as good as any money ... the stamp of full legal tender by the Government is the thing that makes money good any time, and this will always be as good as any other money inside the borders of our country."

33 So that's exactly what Lincoln did. From 1862 to 1865 — with Congressional authorization — he printed $432,000,000 of the new bills.

34 In order to distinguish them from the private bank notes then in circulation, he had them printed with green ink on the back side. That's why the notes were called "Greenbacks."

35 With this new money, Lincoln paid the troops and bought their supplies. During the course of the war, nearly all of the 450 million dollars of Greenbacks authorized by Congress were printed at no interest to the federal government.

36 By now Lincoln realized who was really pulling the strings and what was at stake for the American people. Lincoln under-

stood the matter better than even Jackson apparently had. This is how Lincoln explained his monetary views:

37 *"The Government should create, issue, and circulate all the currency and credit needed to satisfy the spending power of the Government and the buying power of consumers. The privilege of creating and issuing money is not only the supreme prerogative of Government, but it is the Government's greatest creative opportunity.*

38 *"By the adoption of these principles, the long-felt want for a uniform medium will be satisfied. The taxpayers will be saved immense sums of interest. The financing of all public enterprises, and the conduct of the Treasury will become matters of practical administration. Money will cease to be master and become the servant of mankind."*

39 Meanwhile in Britain a truly incredible editorial in the London Times explained the Bank of England's attitude towards Lincoln's Greenbacks.

40 *"If this mischievous financial policy, which has its origin*

in North America, shall become indurated down to a fixture, then the Government will furnish its own money without cost. It will pay off debts and be without debt. It will have all the money necessary to carry on its commerce. It will become prosperous without precedent in the history of the world. The brains and wealth of all countries will go to North America. That country must be destroyed or it will destroy every monarchy on the globe."

41 Keep in mind that by this time the European monarchs were already chained to their private central banks, hence the bankers' concern to preserve their captive monarchs.

42 Within four days of the passage of the law which allowed Greenbacks to be issued, bankers met in convention in Washington to discuss the situation. It was agreed that Greenbacks would surely be their ruin. Something had to be done. They devised a scheme gradually to undermine the value of the Greenbacks.

43 Unimportant limitations on the use of Greenbacks, insisted on by the bankers — forbidding their use to pay import duties and interest on the public debt — were utilized by the banks to justify a surcharge on Greenbacks of up to 185%.

44 This undermined the confidence of the people in Greenbacks and drew further concessions to the bankers to obtain more, discounted as the Greenbacks now were.

45 This scheme was effective - so effective that the next year, 1863, with Federal and Confederate troops beginning to gather for the decisive battle of the Civil War, and the Treasury in need of further Congressional authority at that time to issue more Greenbacks, Lincoln gave in to the pressure, which he thusly described:

46 *"They persist, they have argued me almost blind — I am worse off than St. Paul. He was in a strait between two. I am in a strait between twenty, and they are bankers and financiers."*

47 Lincoln allowed the bankers to push through the National Banking Act of 1863 in exchange for their support for the urgently

needed additional Greenbacks.

48 This act created "National Banks" (hence the "N.A." still in use after National Bank names) and gave them virtually a tax-free status.

49 The new banks also were given the exclusive power to create a new form of money — National Bank Notes. Though Greenbacks continued to circulate, their quantity was limited, and no more were authorized after the war.

50 On June 13, 1863, according to Judge Rutherford's book, *"Vindication"* this letter was sent from the Rothschilds' London office, which does, in fact, accurately assess the National Banking Act of 1863:

51 *"Rothschild Brothers, Bankers, London, June 25th, 1863.*

Messrs Ikleheimer, Morton and Vandergould, No. 3 Wall St., New York, U.S.A.

Dear Sirs:

A Mr. John Sherman has written us from a town in Ohio, U.S.A., as to the profits that may be made in the National Banking business under a recent act of their Congress, a copy of which act accompanies his letter.

52 *"Apparently this act was drawn upon the plan formulated here last summer by the British Bankers Association, and by that Association recommending to our American friends an act that if enacted into law, would prove highly profitable to the banking fraternity throughout the world.*

53 *"Mr. Sherman declares that there has never been such an opportunity for capitalists to accumulate money, as that presented by this act, and that the old plan of State Banks is so unpopular, that the new scheme will, by contrast, be most favorably regarded, notwithstanding the fact that it gives the National Banks an almost absolute control of the nation's finance.*

54 *"'The few who can understand the system,' he says, 'will either be so interested in its profits, or so dependent upon its favors that there will be no opposition from that class, while on the other hand, the great body of people, mentally incapable of comprehending the tremendous advantages that capital derives*

from the system, will bear its burdens without complaint and perhaps without even suspecting that the system is contrary to their interests.'

55 *"Please advise fully as to this matter and also state whether or not you will be of assistance to us, if we conclude to establish a National Bank in the City of New York. If you are acquainted with Mr. Sherman (he appears to have introduced the Banking Act) we will be glad to know something of him. If we avail ourselves of the information he furnished, we will, of course, make due compensation.*

Awaiting your reply, we are
Your respectful servants,
Rothschild Brothers"

56 From this point on, the U.S. money supply would be created in parallel with an equivalent quantity of debt by bankers buying U.S. government bonds, which they will use as reserves for National Bank Notes, the nation's new form of money, instead of by direct debt-free issue by the government, as were Lincoln's Greenbacks.

57 The banks got interest from the government on the bonds and from the borrowers of their Bank Notes — thus almost doubling their interest income. As historian John Kenneth Galbraith explains:

58 *"In numerous years following the war, the Federal government ran a heavy surplus. It could not however pay off its debt, and retire its securities, because to do so would mean that there would be no bonds to back the national bank notes. To pay off the debt would be to destroy the money supply."*

59 Predictably, the new National Banks quickly applied pressure to Congress to have state bank notes taxed out of existence. Congress complied. Thus the fifth American Central Bank War progressed in favor of the Money Changers, culminating in passage of the Federal Reserve Act of 1913 and the National Bank Act of 1935.

60 In 1863, Lincoln got some unexpected help from Czar Alexander II of Russia. The Czar, like Bismarck in Germany, knew what the international Money Changers were up to and had steadfastly refused to grant them authority to set up a privately-

owned central bank in Russia.

61 If America survived and were able to remain out of the clutches of the Federal Reserve Banks, his position would be more secure.

62 If the bankers were successful at dividing America and giving the pieces back to Great Britain and France (both nations by now under control of their privately-owned central banks), eventually they would turn on Russia.

63 So, the Czar gave orders that if either England or France actively intervened and gave aid to the American southern states, Russia would consider such action as a declaration of war.

64 Alexander sent his Pacific fleet under Admiral Popov to port in San Francisco, where it arrived on October 12, 1863, and part of his Baltic fleet under Admiral Lisiviski to port in New York on September 24, 1863, and later to Alexandria, Virginia, which lies across the river from Washington, D.C., as a forceful show of support for Lincoln, and a warning to Britain and France.

65 Further, the Czar was still in a revengeful mood from Russia's defeat in the Crimean War (1853-56) by Money Changer-controlled Britain and France (joined by Turkey and Sardinia).

66 Lincoln was re-elected the next year, 1864. For more Greenbacks, prior to the end of the war, the bankers obtained more concessions in the second National Banking Act, of 1864.

67 Victorious in the Civil War — had Lincoln lived — and as his statements quoted above and following make abundantly clear — he would surely have killed the National Banks' money monopoly extracted from him during the war.

68 On November 21, 1864, Lincoln wrote this to a friend:

69 *"The money power preys upon the nation in times of peace and conspires against it in times of adversity. It is more despotic than monarchy, more insolent than autocracy, more selfish than bureaucracy. I see in the near future a crisis approaching that unnerves me and causes me to tremble for the safety of my country.*

70 *"Corporations have been enthroned, an era of corruption*

in high places will follow, and the money power of the country will endeavor to prolong its reign by working upon the prejudices of the people until the wealth is aggregated in a few hands and the republic is destroyed."

71 Shortly before Lincoln was assassinated, his former Secretary of the Treasury, Salmon P. Chase, bemoaned his role in helping secure the passage of the National Banking Act one year earlier:

72 *"My agency in promoting the passage of the National Banking Act was the greatest financial mistake in my life. It has built up a monopoly which affects every interest in the country."*

73 On April 14, 1865, 41 days after his second inauguration, and five days after Lee surrendered to Grant at Appomattox — though the Civil War was over — Lincoln was shot, while attending Ford's theater, by John Wilkes Booth.

74 Bismarck, the Chancellor of Germany, lamented the death of Abraham Lincoln in these words:

75 *"The death of Lincoln was*

a disaster for Christendom. There was no man in the United States great enough to wear his boots."

76 Bismarck well understood the Money Changers' plan.

77 Allegations that international bankers were responsible for Lincoln's assassination surfaced in Canada 70 years later, in 1934.

78 Gerald G. McGeer, a popular and well-respected Canadian attorney, revealed this stunning charge in a five-hour speech before the House of Commons blasting Canada's debt-based money system. Remember, it was 1934, the height of the Great Depression which was ravaging Canada as well as elsewhere.

79 McGeer had obtained evidence deleted from the public record, provided to him by Secret Service agents, from the trial of John Wilkes Booth, after Booth's death.

80 McGeer said this evidence showed that Booth was a mercenary working for the international bankers.

81 According to an article in the Vancouver Sun of May 2, 1934:

82 *"Abraham Lincoln was as-*

sassinated through the machinations of a group representative of the international bankers, who feared the United States President's national credit ambitions.

83 *"There was only one group in the world at that time who had any reason to desire the death of Lincoln. They were the men opposed to his national currency program and who had fought him throughout the whole Civil War on his policy of Greenback currency."*

84 McGeer claimed that Lincoln was assassinated not only because international bankers wanted to re-establish a central bank in America, but because they also wanted to base America's currency on gold — gold they controlled.

85 In other words, put America on a "gold standard." Silver was to be demonetized, and all Greenbacks retired for gold.

86 Lincoln had done just the opposite by issuing U.S. Notes (Greenbacks) which were based purely on the good faith and credit of the United States.

87 The article quoted McGeer as saying:

88 *"They were the men interested in establishing a gold standard and the right of the bankers to manage the currency and credit of every nation in the world. With Lincoln out of the way they were able to proceed with the plan and did proceed with it in the United States.*

89 *"Within eight years after Lincoln's assassination, silver was demonetized and the gold standard money system set up in the United States."*

90 Not since Lincoln has the U.S. issued debt-free United States Notes. The red-sealed U.S. Notes (Federal Reserve Notes are green-sealed) have been re-issued fourteen (14) times since Lincoln's assassination. They are not new issues, but merely the old Greenbacks reissued year after year as they wear out. Their quantity was eventually limited to $300 million, eventually less than one percent of U.S. currency.

91 In another act of ignorance and folly, the 1994 Riegle Act actually authorized the replacement of Lincoln's Greenbacks with debt-based Federal Reserve Notes. In other words, Lincoln's

Greenbacks were in circulation in the United States until 1994, for 130 years. This was a discovery the bankers wanted carefully buried. They can now be found only in rare currency collections.

92 Why was silver bad for the bankers, and gold good? Simple.

93 Silver was plentiful in the United States, and elsewhere, so it was relatively hard to control. Gold was, and always has been scarce.

94 Throughout history it has been relatively easy to monopolize gold, but silver has historically been 15 times more plentiful.

95 May the grace of our Lord Jesus Christ be with you all. Amen.

CHAPTER 25

WITH Lincoln out of the way, the Money Changers next objective was to gain complete, centralized control over America's money. This was no easy task.

2 With the opening of the American West, silver had been discovered in huge quantities. On top of that, Lincoln's Greenbacks were generally popular and their existence had let the genie out of the bottle — the public was becoming accustomed to debt-free money issued by the government.

3 Despite the European central bankers' deliberate attacks on the Greenbacks, they continued to circulate in the United States.

4 According to author W. Cleon Skousen:

5 *"Right after the Civil War there was considerable talk about reviving Lincoln's brief experiment with the Constitutional monetary system. Had not the European money-trust intervened, it would have no doubt become an established institution."*

6 It is clear that the reality of America printing her own debt-free money sent shock-waves throughout the European private central banking elite. They watched with horror as Americans began to petition for more Greenbacks. They may have killed Lincoln, but support for his monetary ideas grew.

7 On April 12, 1866, nearly one year to the day of Lincoln's assassination, Congress went to work at the bidding of the European central bank interests. It passed the Contraction Act, authorizing the Secretary of the Treasury to begin retiring the Greenbacks in circulation and to contract the money supply.

8 Authors Theodore R. Thoren and Richard F. Warner explained the results of the money contraction in their book on the subject, *The Truth in Money Book:*

9 *"The hard times which occurred after the Civil War could have been avoided if the Greenback legislation had continued as President Lincoln had intended. Instead, there were a series of 'money panics' what we call 'recessions' which put pressure on Congress to enact legislation to place the banking system under centralized control. Eventually the Federal Re-*

serve Act was passed on the 23rd of December, 1913."

10 The Money Changers wanted two things: (1) the re-institution of a privately-owned central bank under their exclusive control, and (2) an American currency issued by them and backed by their gold.

11 Their strategy was two-fold: <u>first</u>, to cause a series of panics to try to convince the American people that the existing decentralized banking system did not work and that only centralized control of the money supply could provide economic stability; <u>secondly</u>, to remove so much money from the system that most Americans would be so desperately poor that they wouldn't be patient enough to fight for true reform, or would be too weak to oppose the bankers, who would offer them relief if the bankers' plans were approved: in short, to convince Americans it was worth the long-term risk to freedom to obtain short-term economic relief.

12 There was $1,800,000,000. in currency in circulation in the United States in 1866. — about $50.46 per capita. More than $500,000,000. was removed from the U.S. money supply in 1867 alone. Ten years later, in 1876, America's money supply was reduced to even less than $600,000,000. In other words, two-thirds of America's money had been called in by the bankers in ten years. Incredibly, only $14.60 per capita remained in circulation.

13 Ten years after that, the money supply had been further reduced to only $400,000,000. even though the population had boomed. The result was that only $6.67 per capita remained in circulation, an 84% decline in just 20 years. The people suffered terribly in a protracted, severe depression.

14 Today, bank-funded economists try to sell the idea that recessions and depressions are a natural part of what they call the "business cycle."

15 One economist actually tried to explain business cycles with reference to sun spots!

16 The truth is, our money supply is completely manipulated, now, just as it was after the Civil War, just as it was by Nicholas Biddle and the second Bank of

the United States.

17 How did money become so scarce? Simple — bank loans were called in and no new bank loans were given. In addition, Greenbacks were retired by the millions and silver coins were melted down.

18 On March 13, 1868, James Rothschild wrote to his U.S. agent, Belmont, *"warning ruin to those who might oppose the payment of U.S. Bonds in coin, or who might advocate their liquidation in greenbacks."* Another scheme was afoot.

19 On March 18, 1869, at these bankers' bidding, Congress passed the Credit Strengthening Act which provided that U.S. bonds purchased during the Civil War with greenbacks that the bankers had discounted on receipt to as little as 35 cents on the dollar, would be repaid in gold at full value.

20 By this means the Treasury paid the bankers some $500 million more than they had paid for the bonds, plus the interest due.

21 A colossal sum, equivalent to well over 5 billion dollars today, was thus transferred from the Treasury to the Money Changers. Thereafter, their power over the U.S. thus mightily augmented continually increased.

22 In 1872, a man named Ernest Seyd was given £100,000 (about $5,000,000 then) by the Bank of England and sent to America to bribe the necessary Congressmen to get silver *demonetized to further reduce the money supply."* He was told that if this was not sufficient, to draw another £100,000, *"or as much more as was necessary."*

23 The next year, Congress passed the Coinage Act of 1873 and the minting of silver dollars abruptly stopped.

24 In fact, Rep. Samuel Hooper, who introduced the bill in the House acknowledged that Mr. Seyd actually drafted the legislation. But it gets worse than that. In 1874, Seyd himself admitted who was behind the scheme:

25 *"I went to America in the winter of 1872-73, authorized to secure, if I could, the passage of a bill demonetizing silver. It was in the interest of those I represented — the governors of the Bank of England — to have it done."*

26 The international bankers accomplished the same demonetization of silver in Germany (1871-73); in the Latin Monetary Union (France, Italy, Belgium, Switzerland) (1873-74); in the Scandinavian Union (Denmark, Norway and Sweden) (1875-76); and in the Netherlands (1875-76).

27 Within five short years, the gold standard was thus imposed worldwide, with China being the only significant holdout.

28 But the contest over control of America's money was not yet over. Only three years later, in 1876, with one-third of America's workforce unemployed, the population was growing restless.

29 People were clamoring for a return to the Greenback Money system of President Lincoln, or a return to silver money — anything that would make money more plentiful. A Greenback Party developed which received over one million votes at its height, as did a strong pro-silver movement.

30 That year, Congress created the United States Silver Commission to study the problem. Their report clearly blamed the mon-etary contraction on the National Bankers. The report is interesting because it compares the deliberate money contraction by the National Bankers after the Civil War, to the Fall of the Roman Empire.

31 *"The disaster of the Dark Ages was caused by decreasing money and falling prices. Without money, civilization could not have had a beginning, and with a diminishing supply, it must languish and finally perish, unless relieved.*

32 *"At the Christian era the metallic money of the Roman Empire amounted to more than $1,800,000,000. by the end of the fifteenth century it had shrunk to $200,000,000 — History records no other such disastrous transition as that from the Roman Empire to the Dark Ages."* (U.S. Silver Commission (1876)).

33 Despite this Silver Commission report, Congress took no action. The next year riots broke out from Pittsburgh to Chicago (1877). The torches of starving vandals lit up the sky.

34 The bankers huddled to decide on their next move. They de-

cided to hang tough. Now that they were back in control of America's money, to a large extent, though not yet to the degree that the second Bank of the United States had been before Jackson killed it, they were not about to give it up.

35 At the meeting of the American Bankers Association that year, they urged their membership to do everything in their power to put down the notion of a return to debt-free Greenbacks.

36 The ABA Secretary, James Buel, authored a letter to the members which blatantly called on the banks to subvert not only Congress, but the press:

37 *"It is advisable to do all in your power to sustain such prominent daily and weekly newspapers (especially the Agricultural and Religious Press) that oppose the greenback issue of paper money, and withhold patronage from all applicants who are not willing to oppose the government issue of money.*

38 *"To repeal the Act creating bank notes, or to restore to circulation the government issue of money will be to provide the people with money and will*

therefore seriously affect our individual profits as bankers and lenders. See your Congressman at once and engage him to support our interests that we may control legislation."

39 As political pressure mounted in Congress for change, the banker influenced press tried to turn the American people away from the truth.

40 The New York Tribune put it this way on January 10, 1878:

41 *"The capital of the country is organized at last, by the National Banks — and we will now see whether Congress will dare to fly in its face."* But this didn't entirely work.

42 On February 28, 1878, Congress passed the Sherman Law allowing the minting of a limited number of silver dollars, ending a five-year hiatus.

43 This did not end gold-backing of the currency, however. Nor did it completely free silver.

44 Prior to 1873, anyone who brought silver to the U.S. mint could have it struck into silver dollars free of charge. No longer.

45 But at least some silver money began to flow back into the economy again. Under politi-

cal pressure, the bankers loosened up on loans for awhile and the post-Civil-War depression was finally ended.

46 Three years later, the American people elected Republican James Garfield President.

47 Garfield understood how the economy was being manipulated.

48 As a Congressman, he had been chairman of the Appropriations Committee, and was a member of the Banking and Currency Committee. After his inauguration, he slammed the Money Changers publicly in 1881:

49 *"Whoever controls the volume of money in any country is absolute master of all industry and commerce ... and when you realize that the entire system is easily controlled, one way or another, by a few powerful men at the top, you will not have to be told how periods of inflation and depression originate."*

50 Garfield understood, and within a few weeks of making this statement, on July 2 of 1881, he was assassinated.

51 May the grace of our Lord Jesus Christ be with you all. Amen.

CHAPTER 26

UNDER the National Banking Act, the Money Changers were gathering strength fast.

2 They began a periodic fleecing of the flock, by creating economic booms, with easy money and loans, followed by busts caused by tight money and fewer loans, so they could buy up thousands of homes and farms for pennies on the dollar on foreclosure.

3 In 1891, the Money Changers prepared to take down the American economy again, and their methods and motives were laid out with shocking clarity in a memo sent out by the American Bankers Association (ABA), an organization in which most bankers were members.

4 This memo called for bankers to create a depression on a certain date three years in the future. Here is how the memo read in part (note the telling reference to England, home of the Mother Bank):

5 *"On Sept, 1, 1894, we will not renew our loans under any consideration. We will demand our money on Sept. 1st . We will foreclose and become mortgag-*

ees in possession. We can take two-thirds of the farms west of the Mississippi, and thousands of them east of the Mississippi as well, at our own price. We may as well own three-fourths of the farms of the West and the money of the country. Then the farmers will become tenants as in England." (American Bankers Association [1891], as printed in the Congressional Record of April 29, 1913).

6 These depressions could be controlled when the National Banks coordinated their contraction; and more easily with America on the gold standard. Gold is one of the easiest commodities to manipulate since it is scarce.

7 People wanted silver money legalized again so they could escape the stranglehold that the Money Changers had on gold-backed money. People wanted Mr. Seyd's Act of 1873 reversed (by then called the Crime of '73) and silver money reinstated.

8 By 1896, the issue of more silver money had become the central issue in the Presidential campaign.

9 William Jennings Bryan, a

Senator from Nebraska ran for President as a Democrat on the "Free Silver" issue. His father had been an ardent Greenbacker.

10 At the Democratic National Convention in Chicago, Bryan made an emotional speech which won him the nomination, entitled, *"Crown of Thorns and Cross of Gold."*

11 Though Bryan was only 36 years old at the time, this speech is widely regarded as the most famous oration ever made before a political convention.

12 In the dramatic conclusion. Bryan said:

13 *"We will answer their demand for a gold standard by saying to them: You shall not press down upon the brow of labor this crown of thorns; you shall not crucify mankind upon a cross of gold."*

14 The bankers lavishly supported the Republican candidate, William McKinley, who favored the gold standard. The resulting contest was among the most fiercely contested Presidential races in American history.

15 Bryan made over 600 speeches in 27 states.

16 Bryan stood with the Greenbackers:

17 *"The right to coin and issue money is a function of Government. It is a part of sovereignty and cannot, with safety, be delegated to private individuals."*

18 The McKinley campaign got manufacturers and industrialists to inform their employees that if Bryan were elected, all factories and plants would close and there would be no work. The ruse succeeded. McKinley beat Bryan by a small margin.

19 Some authors believe, and the course of history supports them, that under the bankers' President, McKinley, before the summer of 1897, the United States entered into a secret agreement (no papers of any sort were signed) that the U.S. would support England in its inevitable conflict with Germany — the product of Bismarck's nation building.

20 This was a de facto agreement surrendering American independence into a worldwide alliance to dominate the world, presided over by the Money Changers who dominated the Bank of England from the City

of London, and through it, the Crown and the British government.

21 Almost immediately, in 1898, the Spanish-American War began. Later, the U.S. was dragged into two World Wars (and other minor wars) to secure the Money Changers' worldwide imperialistic designs.

22 The 1897 Agreement made the U.S. a principal in the British Empire that has been succeeded by the international financial empire of the Money Changers, defended and expanded by the United States, and more recently by the United States led armed forces of the United Nations.

23 Bryan ran for president again in 1900 and in 1908, but fell short both times. But the threat his presence presented to the National Bankers afforded the Republican alternatives, Roosevelt and Taft, a grating measure of independence from the bankers (Roosevelt mildly opposed their monopolies and Taft was unenthusiastic about their proposed central bank legislation), who therefore shifted support to Wilson in 1912.

24 During the 1912 Democratic Convention, Bryan was a powerful figure, and stepped aside to help Woodrow Wilson win the nomination. When Wilson became President he appointed Bryan to be Secretary of State. But Bryan soon became disenchanted with the Wilson administration.

25 Bryan served only two years in the Wilson administration before resigning in 1915 over the highly-suspicious sinking of the Lusitania, the event used to drive America into World War I.

26 Although William Jennings Bryan never gained the Presidency, his efforts delayed the Money Changers for seventeen years from attaining their next goal — a new, privately-owned central bank for America.

27 But like Wilson, Bryan was deceived as to the true import of the Federal Reserve Act of 1913. Both initially supported it. Both later publicly repented over their support of it. Bryan later wrote:

28 *"That is the one thing in my public career that I regret — my work to secure the enactment of the Federal Reserve Law."*

29 May the grace of our Lord Jesus Christ be with you all. Amen.

CHAPTER 27

NOW it was time for the Money Changers to get back a new private central bank for America — the fifth private central bank to control and manipulate America's money supply.

2 A major final panic would be necessary to focus the nation's attention on the supposed need for a central bank.

3 The thin rationale offered was that only a central bank could prevent widespread bank failures and stabilize the currency; but the critically important feature of who would own it, and control it, was a carefully avoided issue.

4 Before the Civil War, the Rothschilds had previously used, as principal agents in the U.S., the J.L. and S.I. Joseph & Company.

5 George Peabody, an American bond salesman, had traveled to London before the Civil War and developed a relationship with Nathan Rothschild, which became a highly profitable one for Peabody. His business expanding, and he took on an American partner, Junius Mor-gan, father of J.P.

6 In 1857 Junius was the recipient of a £800,000 loan from the Bank of England at a time of financial crisis when many other firms were denied such loans.

7 Junius Morgan became the American Union's financial agent in Britain, often closely associated with the Rothschilds.

8 In the post-Civil War period the connection between Morgan and the Rothschilds was certainly well known in financial circles.

9 As one writer noted:

10 *"Morgan's activities in 1895-1896 in selling U.S. gold bonds in Europe were based on his alliance with the House of Rothschild."*

11 After his father's death, J.P. Morgan took on a British partner, Edward Grenfell, a long-time director of the Bank of England.

12 There is speculation that the Morgans became the Rothschilds' principal agents in the U.S., eventually to be eclipsed by the Rockefellers.

13 Early in this century, in U.S. finance, the press, and in politics, all lines of power con-

verged on the financial houses of J.P. Morgan (J.P. Morgan Company; Bankers Trust Company; First National Bank of New York, Guaranty Trust), the Rockefellers (National City Bank of New York; Chase National Bank; Chemical Bank); Kuhn, Loeb & Company (a representative of the Rothschild banks; National City Bank of New York) and the Warburg's (Manhattan Corp. bank).

14 Morgan was clearly the most powerful banker in America, and like his father, worked as an agent for the Rothschild family, but also for his own interests.

15 Morgan helped finance the monopolization of various industries, consolidated big steel holdings into a monopoly by buying Andrew Carnegie's steel companies, and owned numerous industrial companies and banks.

16 Though reputedly America's richest banker, upon J.P.'s death, his estate contained $68 million dollars, only 19% of J.P. Morgan company.

17 The bulk of the securities most people thought he owned, were in fact owned by others.

When Jack P. Morgan, Jr. died in 1943 his estate was valued at only $16 million. By contrast, when Alphonse Rothschild died in 1905 his estate contained $60 million in U.S. securities alone.

18 John D. Rockefeller and his brother William used their enormous profits from the Standard Oil monopoly to dominate the National City Bank, merged in 1955 with Morgan's and Kuhn, Loeb & Company's First National Bank of New York, which resulted in Citibank (Citicorp).

19 Similarly, John D. bought control of Chase National Bank, and merged it with Warburg's Manhattan bank, resulting in the Rockefeller-dominated Chase Manhattan bank, more recently merged with the Rockefeller-controlled Chemical Bank.

20 The combination of the Rockefeller-controlled Chase-Manhattan/Citicorp banks gave them majority control over the New York Fed (52%), which completely dominates the Federal Reserve System.

21 But the New York Fed was controlled by Rockefeller long before any majority ownership was reached.

22 By these mergers, the Rockefellers gradually replaced the Morgans, Schiffs and Warburgs as the principal Rothschild allies in the United States. Recent 1998 mega-bank mergers have further consolidated this monolithic control.

23 David Rockefeller, retired Chairman, was the point man for the Rockefellers in recent decades. One newspaper described the Rockefellers' seventy-five palatial Pocantico Hills residences (on over 4,000 acres) in New York as *"the kind of place God would have built if he had had the money."*

24 In Europe a similar consolidation resulted in two main banking dynasties — the Warburgs and the Rothschilds.

25 But whereas the Morgans and the Rockefellers were relatively fierce competitors until the famous Northern Securities battle resulted in a sort of truce, the Warburgs have always been subordinate to the Rothschilds and have never seriously challenged them.

26 The relationship between the Rothschilds and Rockefellers was initially one of debtor/creditor, as the Rothschild's provided the seed money for J.D. Rockefeller to monopolize the U.S. oil refinery business and most oil production.

27 Subsequently, the relationship entered into measured competition here (local wars between subordinates sometimes resulting), and cooperation there; but like the competition between the other banks, this too was resolved into a power sharing arrangement.

28 The centers of power are not easy to identify, and remain to a large extent hidden through carefully concealed and interlocking directorships, off-shore accounts, nominee holdings, private foundations, trusts, and the rest. But the top international bankers are vested with the last word in economic and political power.

29 Most commentators are of the opinion that the Rothschilds are definitely the dominant partner; citing, for example, the 1950's appointment of J. Richardson Dil-worth, partner of Kuhn, Loeb & Co. (a satellite of the Rothschild family) who left to take control of the Rockefeller

family purse strings, where he managed the investments of Rockefeller descendants in as many as 200 private foundations.

30 However, the operative relationship described by Georgetown historian Carroll Quigley is "feudalistic", that is, analogous to the relationships between a feudal king and the aristocracy consisting of dukes, earls, barons, etc., all mutually supportive, while safeguarding their own turf and "independence", expanding it when permitted without violating the fundamental hierarchical relationships — such violations can result in wars.

31 Lesser members of this "feudalistic" international banking plutocracy include or have included, the Sassoon's (India and the Far East); Lazard Freres (France); Mendelsohn (Netherlands); Israel Moses Seif (Italy); Kuhn, Loeb (U.S.); Goldman Sachs (U.S.) Lehman Bros. (U.S.); Schroeders (Germany) ; Hambros (Scandina-via), the Bethmanns, Ladenburgs, Erlangers, Sterns, Seligmans, Schiffs, Speyers, Abs, Mirabauds, Mallets, Faulds, and many others.

32 The ruling clique in most nations now (excepting a portion of the Muslim world and a few so called "rogue" states) are equivalent to local barons, subservient to the higher banking dukes, earls, etc.

33 This generally reaches right down to the city level, where the dominant local bankers are usually the petty aristocracy, affiliated through banking and commercial relationships with their banking "barons" and so on.

34 As Georgetown University historian Professor Carroll Quigley has noted, if it were possible to detail the asset portfolios of the banking plutocrats one would find the title-deeds of practically all the buildings, industries, farms, transport systems and mineral resources of the world. Accounting for this, Quigley wrote:

35 *"Their secret is that they have annexed from governments, monarchies, and republics the power to create the world's money on debt-terms requiring tribute both in principal and interest."*

36 Unfortunately, rather than benevolent rulers, this interna-

tional banking plutocracy has taken the Malthusian position that the world is overpopulated with serfs; and at the highest levels is deadly serious about correcting this "threat" and "imbalance" whatever the cost in human suffering and misery.

37 To return to 1902: President Theodore Roosevelt allegedly went after Morgan and his friends by using the Sherman Anti-Trust Act to try to break up their industrial monopolies. Actually, Roosevelt did very little to interfere in the growing monopolization of American industry by the bankers and their surrogates.

38 For example, Roosevelt supposedly broke up the Standard Oil monopoly. But it wasn't really broken up at all. It was merely divided into seven corporations, all still controlled by the Rockefellers, who had been originally financed by the Rothschild-controlled National City Bank of Cleveland. The public was aware of this thanks to political cartoonists like Thomas Nash who referred to the bankers as the "Money Trust."

39 By 1907, the year after Teddy Roosevelt's re-election, Morgan decided it was time to try for a central bank again. Using their combined financial muscle, Morgan and his friends were able to crash the stock market that year.

40 Thousands of small banks were vastly overextended. Some of Morgan's principal competitors went under. Some had reserves of less than one percent (1%), thanks to the fractional reserve banking technique.

41 Within days, runs on banks were commonplace across the nation. Now Morgan stepped into the public arena and offered to prop up the faltering American economy by supporting failing banks with money he generously offered to create out of nothing.

42 It was an outrageous proposal, worse than even fractional reserve banking, but, in a panic, Congress let him do it. Morgan manufactured $200 million dollars worth of this totally reserveless, private money — bought things with it, paid for services with it, and sent some of it to his branch banks to lend out at interest.

43 His plan worked. Soon, the

public regained confidence in money in general and quit hoarding their currency. But in the interim, many small banks failed and banking power was further consolidated into the hands of a few large banks.

44 By 1908 the arranged panic was over and Morgan was hailed as a hero by the president of Princeton University, named Woodrow Wilson, who naively wrote:

45 *"All this trouble could be averted if we appointed a committee of six or seven public-spirited men like J.P. Morgan to handle the affairs of our country."*

46 Economic textbooks would later explain that the creation of the Federal Reserve System was the direct result of the panic of 1907.

47 One quote:

48 *"with its alarming epidemic of bank failures: the country was fed up once and for all with the anarchy of unstable private banking."*

49 But Minnesota Congressman Charles A. Lindbergh, Sr., the father of the famous aviator, "Lucky Lindy," later explained that the Panic of 1907 was really just a scam:

50 *"The Money Trust caused the 1907 panic. Those not favorable to the Money Trust could be squeezed out of business and the people frightened into demanding changes in the banking and currency laws which the Money Trust would frame."*

51 Since the passage of the National Banking Act of 1863, the National Banks that the Act established as a cartel, had been able to coordinate a series of booms and busts.

52 The purpose was not only to fleece the American public of their property, but later to claim that the decentralized banking system was basically so unstable that it had to be further consolidated, and control centralized into a central bank once again, as it had been before Jackson ended it.

53 The critical economic issue of private vs. state ownership and control was carefully skirted, as was the fractional reserve banking fraud causing the booms and busts.

.

CHAPTER 28

AFTER the crash, in response to the Panic of 1907, Teddy Roosevelt signed into law a bill creating the National Monetary Commission.

2 The Commission was to study the banking problem and make recommendations to Congress. Of course, the Commission was packed with Morgan's cronies and friends.

3 The Chairman was a man named Senator Nelson Aldrich from Rhode Island.

4 Aldrich represented the Newport, Rhode Island homes of America's richest banking families and was an investment associate of J.P. Morgan, with extensive bank holdings himself.

5 His daughter married John D. Rockefeller, Jr., and together they had five sons: John III; Nelson (who would become the Vice-President of the U.S. in 1974); Laurence; Winthrop; and David (the head of the Council on Foreign Relations and former Chairman of Chase Manhattan bank).

6 As soon as the National Monetary Commission was established, Senator Aldrich immediately embarked on a two-year tour of Europe, where he consulted at length with the private central bankers in England, Germany, and France. The total cost of his trip to the taxpayers was $300,000; a huge sum in those days.

7 Shortly after his return to America, on the evening of November 22, 1910 seven men representing an estimated one-forth of the total wealth of the entire world, boarded Senator Aldrich's sleek, private railroad car at the New Jersey railway station, and in the strictest secrecy journeyed to Morgan's summer estate on Jekyll Island, on the Atlantic seaboard, off the coast of Georgia,

8 Senator Nelson W. Aldrich; Jacob Schiff, Abraham P. Andrew; Frank A. Vanderlip; Henry P. Davison; Charles D. Norwood; Benjamin Strong; and Paul M. Warberg, assembled in secret conclave at the Jekyll Island Hunt Club owned by J. P. Morgan at Jekyll Island, Georgia. In short, all of the international bankers in America — all of them members of the hierarchy of the Great Conspiracy.

9 After ten days of secret meet-

ings during the Thanksgiving Day holiday, while supposedly Duck Hunting in the open air, they emerged on Saturday, December 3, with what they later called the Federal Reserve System.

10 Senator Aldrich was the stooge who was to "railroad" the Federal Reserve Act through Congress, but they held that in abeyance for one chief reason — they first had to plant their man, an obedient stooge, in the White House to sign the Federal Reserve Act into law. They knew that even if the Senate were to pass that Act unanimously, the then newly elected President Taft would promptly veto it, so they had to prepare and wait.

11 Paul Warburg had been given a $500,000 per year salary by the investment firm, Kuhn, Loeb & Company to lobby for passage of a privately-owned central bank in America.

12 Jacob Schiff, the grandson of the man who shared the "Green Shield" house with the Rothschild family in Frankfort, was Warburg's partner in this firm.

13 Schiff, as we'll later find out, was in the process of spend-ing $20,000,000. dollars to finance the overthrow of the Czar of Russia.

14 These three European banking families, the Rothschilds, the Warburgs, and the Schiffs were interconnected by marriage, down through the years, just as were their American banking counterparts, the Morgans, the Rocke-fellers and the Aldriches.

15 The elite group of financiers was embarked on a thousand-mile journey that led them to Raleigh, then to Atlanta, then to Savannah, and finally, to the small town of Brunswick, Georgia.

16 Secrecy was so tight that all seven participants were cautioned to use only first names to prevent servants from learning their identities.

17 Full-time caretakers and servants had been given a vacation, and an entirely new, carefully screened staff was brought in for the occasion to make absolutely sure that none of the servants might recognize by sight the identities of these guests

18 It is difficult to imagine any event in history — including preparations for war — that was shielded from public view with

greater mystery and secrecy, than this event.

19 Years later one participant, Frank Vanderlip, president of Rockefeller's National City Bank of New York and a representative of the Kuhn, Loeb & Company interests, confirmed the Jekyll Island trip in the February 9, 1935 edition of the Saturday Evening Post:

20 *"I was as secretive, indeed, as furtive, as any conspirator. Discovery, we knew, simply must not happen, or else all our time and effort would be wasted. If it were to be exposed that our particular group had got together and written a banking bill, that bill would have no chance whatever of passage by Congress."*

21 The participants came together to figure out how to solve their major problem — how to bring back a privately-owned central bank — but there were other problems that needed to be addressed as well.

22 First of all, the market share of the big national banks was shrinking fast.

23 In the first ten years of the century, the number of U.S. banks had more than doubled to over 20,000. By 1913, only 29% of all banks were National Banks and they held only 57% of all deposits.

24 As Senator Aldrich later admitted in a magazine article:

25 *"Before passage of this Act, the New York bankers could only dominate the reserves of New York. Now, we are able to dominate the bank reserves of the entire county."*

26 Therefore, something had to be done to bring these new banks under their control.

27 As John D. Rockefeller put it: *"Competition is a sin."*

28 Actually, moralists agree that *monopoly abuse* is a sin; but why quibble when there's money to be made.

28 Secondly, the nation's economy was so strong that corporations were starting to finance their expansion out of profits instead of taking out huge loans from large banks.

29 In the first 10 years of the new century 70% of corporate funding came from profits. In other words, American industry was becoming independent of the Money Changers and that trend

had to be stopped.

30 All the participants knew that these problems could be hammered out into a workable solution, but perhaps their biggest problem was a public relations problem — the name of the new central bank.

31 That discussion took place in one of the many conference rooms in the sprawling hotel now known as the "Jekyll Island Club".

32 Aldrich believed that the word "bank" should not even appear in the name. Warburg wanted to call the legislation the "National Reserve Bill" or the "Federal Reserve Bill".

33 The idea here was to give the impression that the purpose of the new central bank was "to stop bank runs" but also to conceal its monopoly character. However, it was Aldrich, the egotistical politician, who insisted it be called the "Aldrich Bill".

34 After ten days of meetings at Jekyll Island, the group dispersed. The new central bank (with twelve branches ultimately) would be similar to the old Banks of the United States. It would eventually claim a monopoly over the national currency and create that money out of nothing but thin air.

35 How does the Fed "create" money out of nothing? It is a "four-step" process; but first a word on bonds.

36 Bonds are simply government I.O.U.s or promises to pay.

37 People buy bonds to get a secure rate of interest. At the end of the term of the bond, the government repays the principal, plus interest (if not paid periodically), and the bond is cancelled and destroyed.

38 There are about 3.6 trillion dollars worth of these bonds at present.

39 Now here is the Fed's money-making process:

40 <u>Step 1</u>. The Fed Open Market Committee approves the purchase of U.S. Bonds on the open market.

41 <u>Step 2</u>. The bonds are purchased by the New York Fed Bank from whoever is offering them for sale on the open market.

42 <u>Step 3</u>. The Fed pays for the bonds with "electronic credits" to the seller's bank, which in turn

credits the seller's bank account. These "electronic credits" are based on nothing tangible; the Fed creates them out of nothing.

43 <u>Step 4</u>. The banks use these fictitious deposits as reserves. They can then loan out ten times the amount of their fictitious reserves to new borrowers, all at interest.

44 In this way, a Fed purchase of, say, a million dollars worth of bonds, gets monetized into more than 10 million dollars in bank deposits.

45 The Fed in effect creates 10% of this totally new money out of nothing, by the stroke of a pen, and the banks create the other 90% out of interest bearing loans.

46 Due to a number of important exceptions to the 10% reserve ratio, many loans require no (0%) reserves at all, making it possible for banks to create many more than ten times the fictitious credit-money they have in "reserve".

47 Then to *decrease* the amount of money in the economy, the process is simply reversed — the Fed sells bonds to the public; and money is withdrawn from the purchaser's local bank. Loaning must then be reduced by ten times the amount of the bonds sold; so a Fed sale of a million dollars in bonds, results in 10 million dollars less money circulating in the economy.

48 So how did the Federal Reform Act of 1913 benefit the bankers whose representatives huddled at Jekyll Island?

49 (1) it totally misdirected banking reform efforts from legitimate solutions.

50 (2) it prevented a legitimate, "debt-free" system of government finance from being repeated — like Lincoln's Greenbacks. Therefore, the bond-based debt-system of government finance, that the bankers forced on Lincoln after he created Greenbacks, was now cast in stone.

51 (3) it gave the bankers the right to create more than 90% of our money supply based on nothing but fractional reserves, which they could loan out at interest.

52 (4) it centralized overall control of our nation's money supply in the hands of but a few men.

53 (5) it established a new pri-

vate U.S. central bank independent of effective political control.

54 The structure is a pure cartel.

55 A cartel is a group of independent businesses which join together to coordinate the production, pricing, or marketing interests of their members.

56 The purpose of a cartel is to reduce competition and thereby increase profitability.

57 This is accomplished through a shared monopoly over their industry which forces the public to pay higher prices for their goods or services than would be otherwise required under free-enterprise competition.

58 As with all cartels, it was created by legislation, and is sustained by the power of government under the deception of protecting the consumer.

59 The Federal Reserve is a cartel that has been legalized to serve private interests at the public's expense.

60 With the non-federal Federal Reserve System in place, the United States Government buys the money that America needs from the Fed at a price that the for-profit Fed establishes and controls.

61 Sixteen years after it's creation, the Fed's "Great Contraction" in the early '30s caused the "Great Depression"; and this power has been enhanced since then, through additional amendments.

62 In order to fool the public into thinking the government retains control, the plan called for the Fed to be run by a Board of Governors appointed by the President and approved by the Senate.

63 But all the bankers have to do is to be sure that their men get appointed to the Board of Governors. That isn't hard. Bankers have money, and money buys influence over politicians.

64 Once the participants left Jekyll Island, their public relations blitz was on.

65 The big New York banks pooled a "educational" fund of $5,000,000. dollars to finance professors at respected universities to endorse the new bank.

66 Woodrow Wilson at Princeton was one of the first professors to jump on the bandwagon.

67 But the bankers' subterfuge didn't work.

68 The Aldrich Bill was quickly identified as a bankers bill — a bill to benefit only what had become known as the "Money Trust."

69 As Congressman Lindbergh put it during the Congressional debate:

70 *"The Aldrich Plan is the Wall Street Plan. It means another panic, if necessary, to intimidate the people. Aldrich, paid by the government to represent the people, proposes a plan for the trusts instead."*

71 Seeing they didn't have the votes to win in Congress, the Republican leadership never brought the Aldrich Bill to a vote.

72 President Taft would not back the Aldrich bill, so the bankers quietly moved to track two, the Democratic alternative.

73 They began financing Woodrow Wilson as the Democratic presidential nominee. He was considered far more tractable than William Jennings Bryan.

74 As historian James Perloff described it:

75 *"Wall Street financier Bernard Baruch was put in charge of Wilson's education. To increase Wilson's chances of defeating the popular Taft, they funded the unwitting Teddy Roosevelt in order to split the Republican vote — a tactic often used since, to insure getting their man in."*

76 On the campaign trail, Roosevelt said:

77 *"Issue of currency should be lodged with the government and be protected from domination by Wall Street. We are opposed to the Aldrich Bill because its provisions would place our currency and credit system in private hands."*

78 This was certainly correct, and it helped draw votes from Taft and got Wilson elected.

79 Since its inception, the Federal Reserve System has presided over the crashes of 1921 and 1929; The Great Depression of 1929-1939; the recessions in 1953, 1957, 1969, 1975, and 1981; the stock market "Black Monday" of 1987; and a 100% inflation which has destroyed 90% of the dollar's purchasing power.

80 By the turn of the century,

an income of $10,000 was required to buy what took only $1,000 in 1914.

81 Corporate debt is soaring; personal debt is greater that ever before; Business and personal bankruptcies are at an all time high; banks and savings associations are failing in larger numbers that even before; interest on the national debt is consuming more that half our tax dollars; heavy industry is being largely replaced by overseas competitors; we are facing an international trade deficit for the first time in our history; 75% of downtown Los Angeles and other metropolitan areas are now owned by foreigners; and more than half of our nation is in a state of economic recession.

82 The System has failed, not because it needs a new set of rules or more intelligent directors, but because it is incapable of achieving its stated objectives.

83 If an institution is incapable of achieving its objectives, there is no reason to preserve it unless it can be altered in some way.

84 When one realizes the circumstances under which it was created, when one contemplates the identities of those who authored it, and when one studies its actual performance over the years, it becomes obvious that the System is simply a cartel with a government facade.

85 May the grace of our Lord Jesus Christ be with you all. Amen.

CHAPTER 29

DURING the Presidential campaign, the Democrats were careful to pretend to oppose the Aldrich Bill.

2 As Rep. Louis McFadden, himself a Democrat as well as chairman of the House Banking and Currency Committee, explained it twenty years after the fact:

3 *"The Aldrich bill was condemned in the platform when Woodrow Wilson was nominated. The men who ruled the Democratic party promised the people that if they were returned to power there would be no central bank established here while they held the reins of government.*

4 *"Thirteen months later that promise was broken, and the Wilson administration, under the tutelage of those sinister Wall Street figures who stood behind Colonel House, established here in our free country the worm-eaten monarchical institution of the 'king's bank' to control us from the top downward, and to shackle us from the cradle to the grave."*

5 Once Wilson was elected, Warburg, Baruch, & company advanced a supposed "new" plan, which Warburg named the Federal Reserve System.

6 The Democratic leadership hailed the new bill — called the "Glass-Owen" Bill — as radically different from the "Aldrich Bill"; but the bill was virtually identical in every important detail.

7 In fact, so vehement were the Democratic denials of similarity to the Aldrich Bill that Paul Warburg — the father of both bills — had to step in privately to reassure his paid friends in Congress that the two bills were virtually the same:

8 *"Brushing aside the external differences affecting the 'shells,' we find the 'kernels' of the two systems closely resembling and related to one another."*

9 But that admission was for private consumption only. Publicly, the Money Trust trotted out Senator Aldrich and Frank Vanderlip — the president of the Morgan/Rockefeller dominated National City Bank of New York and one of the Jekyll Island seven — to offer token opposition to

the new Federal Reserve System.

10 Many years later, Vanderlip admitted in the Saturday Evening Post that the two measures were virtually the same. (Saturday Evening Post, February 9, 1935, page 25, entitled *"From Farmboy to Financier"*).

11 *"Although the Aldrich Federal Reserve Plan was defeated when it bore the name Aldrich, nevertheless its essential points were all contained in the plan that was finally adopted."*

12 As Congress neared a vote, they called Ohio attorney Alfred Crozier to testify.

13 Crozier noted the similarities between the Aldrich Bill and the Glass-Owen Bill:

14 *"The bill grants just what Wall Street and the big boys for twenty five years have been striving for — private instead of public control of currency. It* (the Glass-Owen bill) *does this as completely as the Aldrich Bill.*

15 *"Both measures rob the government and the people of all effective control over the public's money, and vests in the banks exclusively the dangerous power to make money* among the people scarce or plenty."

16 Exactly: During the debate on the measure, Senators complained that the big banks were using their financial muscle to influence the outcome.

17 *"There are bankers in this country who are enemies of the public welfare,"* declared one Senator. What an understatement!

18 Despite the charges of deceit and corruption, the bill was finally rammed through the House and Senate on December 23, 1913, after many Senators and Representatives had left town for the Christmas holidays, having been assured by the leadership that nothing would be done until long after the Christmas recess. On the day the bill was passed, Congressman Lindbergh prophetically warned his countrymen that:

19 *"This Act establishes the most gigantic trust on earth. When the President signs this bill, the invisible government by the Monetary Power will be legalized. The people may not know it immediately, but the day of reckoning is only a few years removed. The worst legislative*

crime of the ages is perpetrated by this banking bill."

20 On top of all this, only weeks earlier Congress had finally passed a bill supposedly legalizing the income tax. (This bill was never ratified).

21 Why was this income tax law important? because bankers finally had in place a system which would run up a virtually unlimited federal debt. So how would the interest on this debt be repaid, not to mention the principal?

22 Remember, a privately-owned central bank creates the principal out of nothing. The federal government was small then. Up to that time, it had subsisted on excise taxes and tariffs.

23 Just as with the Bank of England, the interest payments had to be guaranteed by direct taxation of the people.

24 The Money Changers knew that if they had to rely on contributions from the states, the state legislatures would eventually revolt and either refuse to pay the interest on their own money, or at least bring political pressure to bear to keep the debt small.

25 In 1895 the Supreme Court had found a similar income tax law to be unconstitutional.

26 The Supreme Court even found a corporate income tax law unconstitutional in 1909.

27 Regardless, in October of 1913 Senator Aldrich hustled a bill through the Congress for a constitutional amendment supposedly allowing the income tax.

28 The proposed 16th Amendment to the Constitution was then sent to the state legislatures for approval — but many critics claim that the 16th Amendment was never passed by the necessary 3/4ths of the states.

29 In other words, the 16th Amendment is possibly illegal; but the Money Changers were in no mood to debate its points.

30 Without the power to directly tax the people — bypassing the states, — the Federal Reserve Bill would be less useful to those who wanted to drive America deeply into their debt.

31 A year after passage of the Federal Reserve Bill, Congressman Lindbergh explained how the Fed created what we have come to call the "business cycle" and how they use it to their advantage:

32 *"To cause high prices, all the Federal Reserve Board will do will be to lower the rediscount rate, producing an expansion of credit and a rising stock market; then when business men are adjusted to these fluid conditions, it can check prosperity in mid-career by arbitrarily raising the interest rate.*

33 *"It can cause the pendulum of a rising and falling market to swing gently back and forth by slight changes in the discount rate, or cause violent fluctuations by a greater rate variation, and in either case it will possess inside information as to financial conditions and advance knowledge of the coming change, either up or down.*

34 *"This is the strangest, most dangerous advantage ever placed in the hands of a special privilege class by any Government that ever existed.*

35 *"They will know in advance when to create panics to their advantage. They will also know when to stop panic. Inflation and deflation work equally well for them when they control finance."*

36 Congressman Lindbergh was

correct on all points.

37 What he didn't realize was that most European nations had already fallen prey to the private central bankers, decades or even centuries earlier.

38 But Lindburgh also mentions the fact that only one year later, the Fed had cornered the market in gold. He said:

39 *"Already the Federal Reserve banks have cornered the gold and gold certificates."*

40 Congressman Louis Mc-Fadden, the Chairman of the House Banking and Currency committee (1920-1931) remarked that the Federal Reserve Act established:

41 *"A super state controlled by international bankers and international industrialists acting together to enslave the world for their own pleasure."*

42 Notice how McFadden saw the international character of the stockholders of the Federal Reserve.

43 Another chairman of the House Banking and Currency Committee in the 1960s, Wright Patman from Texas, put it this way:

44 *"In the United States today*

we have in effect two governments. We have the duly constituted Government, then we have
an independent, uncontrolled
and uncoordinated government
in the Federal Reserve System,
operating the money powers
which are reserved to Congress
by the Constitution."

45 Even the inventor of the
electric light, Thomas Edison,
joined the fray in criticizing the
system called the Federal Reserve:

46 *"If our nation can issue a
dollar bond, it can issue a dollar bill. The element that makes
the bond good, makes the bill
good. It is absurd to say that our
country can issue $30 million in
bonds and not $30 million in
currency. Both are promises to
pay. But one promise fattens the
usurers, and the other promise
helps the people."*

47 Three years after the passage of the Federal Reserve Act,
even President Wilson began to
have second thoughts about what
he had unleashed during his first
term in office as president.

48 *"We have come to be one
of the worst ruled, one of the
most completely controlled gov-*
ernments in the civilized world
— no longer a government of
free opinion, no longer a government by a vote of the majority, but a government by the
opinion and duress of a small
group of dominant men.

49 *"Some of the biggest men
in the United States, in the field
of commerce and manufacture,
are afraid of something. They
know that there is a power somewhere so organized, so subtle,
so watchful, so interlocked, so
complete, so pervasive, that
they had better not speak above
their breath when they speak in
condemnation of it."*

50 Before his death in 1924,
President Wilson realized the
full extent of the damage he had
done to America, when he sadly
confessed:

51 *"I have unwittingly ruined
my government."*

52 So finally, the Money Changers — those who profit by creating and manipulating the amount
of money in circulation — had
their privately owned central
bank installed once again in
America.

53 The major newspapers
(which they owned or heavily in-

fluenced through advertising) hailed passage of the Federal Reserve Act of 1913, telling the public that *"now depressions could be scientifically prevented."*

54 The fact of the matter was that now depressions could be scientifically initiated.

55 By bribery, deceitful political manipulation, and abuse of their influence with and ownership of the press, they had usurped the monetary function of the government.

56 The U.S. government was left with only trivial relics of its sovereign monetary power — the minting of coins (a tiny fraction of the money supply but a debt-free fraction); the re-printing of Lincoln's U.S. notes (Greenbacks limited to $300,000,000. total); and issuing a limited number of gold and silver certificates.

57 As Mr. James Rand, former President of Remington Rand, Inc. well said:

58 *"No government should permit such coercive power over its own credit to be held by any one group or class as the privately owned Federal Reserve System holds today.*

59 *"No government should delegate to private interests the control over the purchasing power of money.*

60 *"The issue must be faced and settled. There can be no complete restoration of confidence until the conflict between private and government control over money is ended."*

61 The 5th American Central Bank War ended in victory for the Money Changers; and in defeat for the American people, as a whole.

62 Since then, the Money Changers' grip has gradually tightened year by year, hiding this history and propagandizing the people to support the system's various activities through their media control, thereby choking our liberties by degrees.

63 May the grace of our Lord Jesus Christ be with you all. Amen.

CHAPTER 30

NOW it was time for a war; a really big war, in fact, — the First World War.

2 Nothing creates debt like war, as the central bankers knew.

3 During the 119 year period between the founding of the Bank of England and Napoleon's defeat, at Waterloo, England had been at war for almost half of that time. And for much of the other half of that time she'd been preparing for war.

4 In World War I, the Rothschilds in Germany loaned money to the Germans, the Rothschilds in Britain loaned money to the British, and the Rothschilds in France loaned money to the French.

5 This was all highly profitable.

6 In America, J.P. Morgan was the agent for selling war materials to both the British and the French.

7 In fact, six months into the war, Morgan became the largest consumer on earth — spending $10,000,000 dollars a day.

8 His offices at 23 Wall Street were mobbed by brokers and salesmen trying to cut a deal.

9 In fact, it got so bad that the bank had to post guards at every door and at the partners' homes as well.

10 Other Rothschild allies in the United States prospered equally as well from the war.

11 President Wilson appointed Bernard Baruch to head the War Industries Board.

12 According to historian Jarnes Perloff, both Bernard Baruch and the Rockefellers profited by some $200,000,000. dollars during the war.

13 But profits were not the only motive. There was also power and revenge.

14 The Money Changers never forgave the Russian Czars for their opposition to central banks, nor for supporting Lincoln during the Civil War.

15 Russia was the last major European nation to refuse to give in to the privately-owned central bank scheme.

16 Three years after World War I broke out in 1914, the Russian Revolution (1917) toppled the Czar.

17 Jacob Schiff of Kuhn, Loeb & Company bragged on his deathbed that he had spent $20,000,000 dollars towards the

defeat of the Czar.

18 But the truth was, that much of that money funded the communist coup d'etat that replaced the democratically elected Kerensky regime, which had replaced the Czar, months earlier.

19 The bankers were not so much enemies of the Czar, as they were intent on seizing power in Russia through the Bolsheviks.

20 Three gold shipments in 1920 alone, from Lenin to Kuhn, Loeb & Company and Morgan Guaranty Trust repaid the $20 million to the bankers, and this was but a small down payment.

21 But would some of the richest men in the world financially back communism? the system that was openly vowing to destroy the capitalism that made them wealthy?

22 Communism — like plutocracy — is a *product* of capitalism!

23 Researcher Gary Allen explained it this way:

24 *"If one understands that socialism is not a share-the-wealth program, but is in reality a method to consolidate and control the wealth, then the seeming paradox of super-rich men promoting socialism becomes no paradox at all. Instead, it becomes logical, even the perfect tool for power-seeking megalomaniacs. Communism or more accurately, socialism, is not a movement of the downtrodden masses, but of the economic elite."*

25 As W. Cleon Skousen puts it in his 1970 book *The Naked Capitalist:*

26 *"Power from any source tends to create an appetite for additional power. It was almost inevitable that the super-rich would one day aspire to control not only their own wealth, but the wealth of the whole world. To achieve this, they were perfectly willing to feed the ambitions of the power-hungry political conspirators who were committed to the overthrow of all existing governments and the establishment of a central world-wide dictatorship."*

27 But what if these revolutionaries get out of control and try to seize power from the Money Changers?

28 After all, it was Mao Tsetung who in 1938 stated his position concerning power:

29 *"Political power grows out of the barrel of a gun."*

30 The London/Wall Street axis elected to take the risk.

31 The master-planners attempted to control revolutionary communist groups by feeding them vast quantities of money when they obeyed, and contracting their money supply, or even financing their opposition, or fascist parties in bordering nations, if they got out of control.

32 Lenin began to understand that although he was the dictator of the new Soviet Union, he was not pulling the financial strings, someone else was silently in control:

33 *"The state does not function as we desired. The car does not obey. A man is at the wheel and seems to lead it, but the car does not drive in the desired direction. It moves as another force wishes."*

34 Who was behind it?

35 Rep. Louis T. McFadden, the Chairman of the House Banking and Currency Committee throughout the 1920s and into the Great Depression years of the 1930s, explained it this way:

36 *"The course of Russian history has, indeed, been greatly affected by the operations of international bankers. The Soviet Government has been given United States Treasury funds by the Federal Reserve Board.*

37 *"Acting through the Chase Bank England has drawn money from us through the Federal Reserve banks and has re-lent it at high rates of interest to the Soviet Government.*

38 *"The Dnieper-Story Dam was built with funds unlawfully taken from the United States Treasury by the corrupt and dishonest Federal Reserve Board and the Federal Reserve banks."*

39 In other words, the Fed and the Bank of England, along with their controlling stock-holders, the Rothschilds, the Rockefellers, the Morgans, the Schiffs, the War-burgs, etc., were creating a monster; one which would fuel seven decades of unprecedented Communist revolution, warfare, and most importantly, debt.

40 The Soviet Union was *also* a useful counterbalance to Germany, and later, to the United States, until 1989 when it was

dismembered into fifteen countries.

41 China then became a new counterbalance to the U.S., and is being built up at the rate of over $100 million dollars a day by lopsided trade deals, IMF loans, and Western investments.

42 Such balance-of-power arrangements assure that the Money Changers cannot be overthrown worldwide by a political revolt in any single country.

43 In that case, they would simply shift support to the counterbalancing country.

44 Additionally, the inevitable military rivalry between roughly balanced powers results in massive expenditures and so more national borrowing and debt.

45 In case one thinks there is some chance that the Money Changers got communism going and then lost control, keep in mind that even in the socialist paradise, Rockefeller's National City Bank (now Citigroup) in St. Petersburg, was never nationalized; as were all other Russian banks.

46 Numerous Western bankers operated openly in the Soviet Union and made vast profits.

47 However, setbacks, some major, did occur.

48 For instance, it is likely that early on the bankers preferred the more compliant Mensheviks to the more independent Bolsheviks, but Lenin got the upper hand.

49 But both groups had the same end and so this was not a fundamental division.

50 However, it did lead to a serious problem when Lenin died, because an even more independent sort — Stalin — squeezed out the bankers' candidate, Leon Trotzky (real name: Bronstein, whose wife was linked to the Warburgs), and took control of Soviet Communism.

51 Even then, Stalin continued to fear Trotzky's powerful connections, and so had him tracked down, and eventually assassinated in Mexico.

52 To pressure Stalin back into the ranks, as C.G. Rakovsky explained, the bankers financed Hitler, who was an avowed enemy of communism and openly advocated invading the Soviet Union.

53 Anthony C. Sutton and others have documented the money

trail from Wall Street to Hitler, mentioned above, by Congressman McFadden.

54 It was only on the death of Stalin, with the rise of Khruschev et seq., that the Soviet Union was fully back in the ranks, securely under the bankers' control, — Stalin was murdered.

55 In 1992, The Washington Times reported that Russian President Boris Yeltsen was upset that most of the incoming foreign aid was being siphoned off *"straight back into the coffers of Western banks in debt service."*

56 Much of that debt was incurred under the prior communist regimes, which were heavily in debt to the Money Changers.

57 Similarly, once in power, Mao Tse-Tung spread his wings and expelled the Soviets from Red China leading to the Sino-Soviet rift of the 1960's.

58 The U.S. and the U.S.S.R. initiated an encirclement policy of China including: heavy Soviet troop concentrations and border provocations in Manchuria; drawing North Korea and Mongolia tightly into the Soviet camp; placing nuclear weapons in Manchuria; arming Tibetan freedom fighters and Taiwanese troops; and establishing important U.S. (now Soviet) air and naval bases in Vietnam (such as Cam Rahn Bay) while beefing up U.S. forces in Guam, Japan, Laos and Thailand, all under the pretext of the Vietnam War.

59 Under this growing pressure, Mao first responded with internal political purges, just as Stalin had done, but with the failure of the Great Leap Forward and with the U.S./U.S.S.R. noose tightening, Mao blinked, and Kissinger was sent in to strike the deal.

60 Still, Mao's price for China's cooperation and integration in the bankers' one-world scheme was obviously high.

61 Here is the result: the encirclement ended, including U.S. abandonment of South Vietnam and Laos; China got Taiwan's U.N. seat (and doubtless a pledge of eventually getting Taiwan itself); a free hand in Tibet and Hong Kong; and gigantic bribes in the form of Western development of China.

62 This left the Bankers with few obstacles worldwide: Mus-

lim fundamentalism here and there; India's nuclear development; and the weak remnants of Western nationalism — concentrated in the large but rapidly shrinking U.S. middle class, and in a minority of the British, French, and Russian aristocracy (e.g. Thatcher and Le Pen).

63 To overcome these, the Russian Empire was dismembered into fifteen nations; the U.K, France and the U.S.A. are gradually being submerged into regional and global entities (such as NAFTA, WTO, MAI, EEC, EU, etc.); and Desert Storm and the war in Iraq et seq are keeping the Muslims on a tight leash; while India is being pressured to abandon its nuclear program.

64 The bankers' three main regional groupings: the European Union; the proposed American Union in the Western hemisphere; and Chinese dominance in Asia, are rapidly bringing to life Orwell's three virtually identical world nations set forth in his prophetic book 1984: "<u>Eurasia</u>", "<u>Oceania</u>" and "<u>East Asia</u>" — all set to engage in "perpetual war = perpetual peace" — WWIII — with its attendant debt

and population reduction and control.

65 Orwell got this idea from James Burnham's book *The Managerial Revolution.*

66 Wars are complex things with many causative factors.

67 But on the other hand, it would be equally foolish to ignore, as a prime cause of World Wars I and II, those who would profit the most from war, both financially and politically.

68 Senator Nye of North Dakota raised the possibility that the Wilson administration entered WWI, at a critical juncture for the allies, in order to protect huge Wall Street bank loans to the allies.

69 During the War the U.S. money supply was doubled, to pay for it, halving the dollar's purchasing power and also Americans' savings.

70 The most belligerent prowar hawk surrounding President Wilson was a man named Colonel Edward Mandell House, the son of a man commonly believed to be a Roths-child agent, who was himself closely associated with Wall Street and European bankers.

71 The role of the Money Changers is no wild conspiracy theory.

72 They had a motive — a short-range, self-serving motive, as well as a long-range, political motive — advancing totalitarian government, with the Money Changers maintaining the financial clout to control whatever politicians might emerge as the leaders.

73 Next, we'll see what the Money Changers' political goal for the world is. We must learn from our history before it is too late.

74 May the grace of our Lord Jesus Christ be with you all. Amen.

CHAPTER 31

ALL of our money is created out of debt; it is a debt-money system.

2 Our money is created initially by the purchase of bonds that some day have to be repaid.

3 The public buys bonds, like savings bonds; the banks buy bonds; foreigners buy bonds; and when the Fed wants to create more money in the system, it buys bonds — but pays for them with simple book keeping entries which it creates out of nothing.

4 Then this new money created by the Fed is multiplied by a factor of 10 by the banks, per the fractional reserve principle.

5 So, Although the banks don't create currency per se, they do create check-book money by the stroke of a key, or deposit accounts by making new loans.

6 The Fed even invests some of this money that it creates out of thin air.

7 In fact, over one-trillion dollars of this privately created money has been used to purchase bonds on the open market, which provides the banks with roughly 50 billion! dollars in risk free interest each year, less the mi-

nor interest banks pay to depositors.

8 In this way, through fractional reserve lending, the banks create over 90% of the money supply and therefore almost all of our inflation.

9 What can we do about this?

10 Fortunately there is a way to fix this, fairly easily; speedily; and without any serious financial problems.

11 We can get our country totally out of debt in one to two years by simply paying off these U.S. Bonds with debt-free U.S. Notes, just like Lincoln issued to pay for the Civil War.

12 Of course this by itself, would create tremendous inflation, since our currency is presently multiplied by a factor of 10 by the fractional reserve banking system; but there is a simple solution, advanced in part by economist Milton Friedman, to keep the money supply stable and avoid inflation and deflation while the debt is being retired.

13 As the Treasury buys back it's bonds on the open market, interest free, with U.S. Notes, the reserve requirement of your home town banks would be pro-

portionately raised so the amount of money in circulation would remain constant.

14 As those holding bonds are paid off in U.S. Notes they would deposit this money, thus making available the currency needed by the banks to increase their reserves.

15 Once the U.S. Bonds are replaced with U.S. Notes, banks would be at 100% reserve banking, instead of the fractional reserve system currently in use today.

16 From this point on, the former Fed buildings would only be needed as a central clearing house for checks, and as vaults for the U.S. Notes.

17 The Federal Reserve Act would no longer be necessary and could be repealed.

18 Monetary power would be transferred from the Fed to the Treasury Department.

19 There would be no further creation or contraction of the money supply by the banks.

20 By doing it this way, our national debt would be paid off in a single year or so, and the Fed and fractional reserve banking abolished, without national bank-ruptcy, financial collapse, inflation or deflation, or any significant change in the way the average American goes about his business.

21 To the average person, the result would be that for the first time since the Federal Reserve Act was passed in 1913, taxes would begin to go down, until no longer needed at all, as a real blessing to the average American.

22 May the grace of our Lord Jesus Christ be with you all. Amen.

CHAPTER 32

NOW, let's take a look at these proposals in more detail with a Money Reform Act in mind — variations, with the same results, would be equally welcome of course.

1 Step 1. Pay off the national debt with debt-free U.S. Notes (or Treasury department credits convertible to U.S. Notes). As Thomas Edison put it, if the U.S. can issue a dollar bond, it can issue a dollar bill. They both rest purely on the good faith and credit of the U.S. This amounts to a simple substitution of one type of government obligation for another. One bears interest, the other does not. Federal Reserve Notes could be used for this as well, but could not be printed after the Fed is abolished, as we propose, so we suggest using U.S. Notes instead, as Lincoln did.

2 Step 2. Abolish Fractional Reserve Banking. As the debt is paid off, the reserve requirements of all banks and financial institutions would be raised proportionally at the same time to absorb the new U.S. Notes and prevent inflation, which would be deposited and become the banks' increased reserves. At the end of the first year, or so, all of the national debt would be paid, and we could start enjoying the benefits of full-reserve banking. The Fed would be obsolete, an anachronism. This same approach would work equally well in Canada, England and in virtually all debt-based, central bank controlled economies.

3 Step 3. Repeal of the Federal Reserve Act of 1913 and the National Banking Act of 1864. These acts delegate the money power to a private banking monopoly. They must be repealed and the monetary power handed back to the government (in the U.S., the Department of the Treasury), where they were initially, under President Abraham Lincoln. No banker or person in any way affiliated with financial institutions should be allow to regulate banking. After the first two reforms, these Acts would serve no useful purpose anyway, since they relate to a fractional reserve banking system.

4 Step 4. Withdraw the U.S. from the IMF, the BIS and the World Bank. These institutions,

like the Federal Reserve, are designed to further centralize the power of the international bankers over the world's economy, so the U.S. must withdraw from them or lose its sovereignty and independence. The harmless, useful functions they supply, such as currency exchange, can be accomplished either nationally, or in new organizations limited to those functions.

5 Issuing debt-free currency, not tied to bond issues, is not a radical solution. It's been advocated in its parts by Presidents Jefferson, Madison, Jackson, Van Buren and Lincoln. It's been used at different times in Europe as well.

6 One current example is one of the small islands in the English Channel off the coast of France.

7 Guernsey has been using issues of debt-free money for nearly 200 years to pay for large building projects.

8 Guernsey is an example of just how well a debt-free money system can, and will work.

9 In 1815, a committee was appointed to investigate how best to finance a new market.

10 The impoverished island could not afford more new taxes, so the State's fathers decided to issue their own paper money.

11 They were just colorful paper notes backed by nothing, but the people of this tiny island agreed to accept them and trade with them anyway.

12 To ensure that they circulated widely, they were declared to be "good for the payment of taxes."

13 Of course this idea was nothing new. It was exactly what the colonists in America had done before the American Revolutionary War, and there are other examples of this being done throughout the world.

14 But this was new to Guernsey, and it worked. The market is still in use, and it was built with no debt to the people of this island state.

15 But what if America follows Guernsey's example?

16 The resulting advantages would include: (1) no more bank runs; (2) bank failures would be very rare; (3) the national debt would be entirely paid-off; (4) the monetary, banking, and tax systems would be more efficient, and simplified; (5) significant

inflation and deflation would be eliminated; (6) booms and busts would become insignificant; and (7) banker control of our industry and political life would end.

17 How would the bankers react to these reforms?

18 Certainly the international bankers' cartel would oppose all reforms that do away with their control of the world's economies — as they have in the past.

19 But it is equally certain that Congress has the Constitutional authority and the responsibility to authorize the issuance of debt free money — U.S. Notes, — the same as Lincoln's Greenbacks — and to reform the very banking laws it enacted on ill advice.

20 Undoubtedly, the bankers will claim that issuing debt-free money will cause severe inflation or make other dire predictions, but remember the culprit — *fractional reserve banking* is the cause of almost all inflation — not whether debt-free U.S. Notes are used to pay for the government's cost.

21 The simultaneous transition to full reserve banking will absorb the new notes, thus preventing inflation, while stabilizing banking, and the economy as well.

22 In the current system, any spending excesses on the part of Congress, are turned into more U.S. debt bonds.

23 The 10% of bonds purchased by the Fed, that provide the liquidity in the capital markets needed to purchase the remainder of the new bonds, is multiplied ten times by the bankers, causing most of the inflation we see.

24 Educate yourself and your friends.

25 *"When you know a thing, recognize that you know it, and when you do not — know that you do not know: this is knowledge."* (Confucius).

26 *"You shall know the truth, and the truth shall make you free."* (Jesus of Nazareth, the Bible, NKJV at John 8:32).

27 Our country needs a solid group who really understand how our money is manipulated and what the solutions are, because if a depression comes, friends of the bankers will come forward advancing so-called solutions framed by the bankers.

28 Beware of calls to return to

a gold standard. Why?

29 Simple; because never before has so much gold been so concentrated in foreign hands.

30 Never before has so much gold been in the hands of international government bodies such as the World Bank and International Monetary Fund.

31 In fact, the IMF now holds more gold than any central bank in the world.

32 The Swiss are under intense pressure from the Money Changers to dispose of their gold.

33 This is most likely either a prelude to the complete demonetization of gold (like silver before it), or to its monopolization and re-monetization by the Money Changers.

34 Therefore, to return to a gold standard would almost certainly be a false solution in our case. As we said in the Great Depression: *"In gold we trusted; by gold we were busted."*

35 Likewise, beware of any plans advanced for a regional or world currency — this is an international banker's Trojan Horse — a deception to open the national gates to more international control.

36 Educate your members of Congress; it only takes a few persuasive members of Congress to make the others pay attention.

37 Most Congressmen just don't understand the system.

38 Some Congressmen understand the system, but are influenced by their bank stock ownership, or bank PAC contributions to look the other way, not realizing the gravity of their ignorance and neglect.

39 There is little opportunity for significant monetary reform at present.

40 But if an opportunity ever presents itself, perhaps in a crisis, they at least will have been given the information needed to avoid floundering in banker-induced confusion — as did many reform-minded Congressmen during the Great Depression.

41 We pray that this coverage has made a useful contribution to the national debate on monetary reform.

42 It remains for each of us to do his duty, consistent with our status in life.

43 May God give us the light to help reform our nation and ourselves.

44 We say ourselves: because ultimately vast numbers of us are going to be driven more and more to desperation by the accumulation of the world's wealth in fewer and fewer hands.

45 We will be tempted to become like our oppressors, selfish and greedy. Rather, let's keep in mind this warning to not lose sight of the greater things.

46 As Jesus of Nazareth put it ages ago:

47 *"For what will it profit a man if he gains the whole world, and loses his own soul?"*

Afterword

CHAPTER 33

AND *he causeth all, both small and great, free and bond, to receive a mark in their right hand, or in their foreheads: that no man might buy or sell, save he that had the mark, or the name of the beast, or the number of his name."* — *Rev. 13:16,17.*

2 "The mark, or the name of the beast" is the *trademark* or *trade-name* of the *all capital letter strawman* that the government deals with directly, instead of dealing with you.

3 Your strawman's *birthdate* on his birth certificate is the date when your *all capital letter, govern-ment created trademark/trade-name* was *berthed like a vessel* by the State.

4 Your strawman's *trademark/ tradename* doesn't belong to you; it belongs to your *artificial, vessel strawman.*

5 Your strawman's *birthdate* is the means by which you are *enticed* to be the *surety* for him — by which you are fooled into claiming *his* "berthdate" to be *yours.*

6 This is why you cannot speak for yourself in court. You must have a lawyer speak for you instead — *because you have told this lie.*

7 You *perjure yourself* when you state the date that you were born.

8 Evidence based on something that you were told is *hearsay* that is not recognized by the court.

9 Yes. You were physically present when you were born. But you were too young to know the date or the time first hand.

10 *To be acceptable, evidence must be witnessed to first hand.*

11 You also lie when you *"solemnly swear to tell the truth".* Your *birthdate claim* brings all of your subsequent testimony into question even when you profess to know and swear to tell the truth.

12 What's more: The government doesn't **want** you to tell the truth; it couldn't control you if you did.

13 **The government isn't based on truth.** The government is based on agreement contracts.

14 The "number of his name" is the *number* of your *strawman's name,* — the *number* of his *Social Security Account.*

15 You will find your

strawman's *all capital letter, trademark/trade-name* on his driver's license; on his bank account; on his telephone bills; on his power bills — on all the public papers that are addressed to your *government created, strawman* —not to you.

16 All of these *documents* that you think refer to you are not yours. These *documents* belong to your *ens legis, fictional vessel, strawman.*

17 ***Welcome to the Wonderful World of Oz!***

CHAPTER 34

A N Allegory is the expression of truths about human conduct and experience by means of symbolic fictional figures and actions.

2 Such is the Movie, *The Wizard of Oz,* an allegory of the state of affairs we now live in today;

3 ...an allegory of the unfolding *New World Order* that was instituted in America via the financial meltdown of 1929 and the bankruptcy of the federally owned corporate United States in 1933.

4 The setting of this allegory is in *Kansas;* the "heartland" of America; the geographical center of the U.S.A.

5 In came the twister — the whirling distraction of the stockmarket crash, the Great Depression, and the theft of America's gold — that whisked Dorothy and Toto up into the *New Money Order* of the world; an artificial new dimension *"somewhere, over the rainbow"* beyond the solid ground of Kansas.

6 When they landed in Oz, Dorothy said *rhetorically* to her little dog Toto;

7 *"Toto? I have a feeling we're not in Kansas anymore."*

8 Exactly!

9 After the bankruptcy of the United States, Kansas was no longer "Kansas" anymore, it is now "KS" — a two-capital-letter federal postal designation that is part of the "federal zone" designated by the Zone ImProvement code (ZIP code) established by the bankrupt United States in 1933; and Dorothy and Toto were now *"in this state."*

10 The terms: *"in this state," "this state,"* and *"STATE OF...."* are deceptively defined for jurisdictional purposes as part of the "DISTRICT OF COLUMBIA OR THE UNITED STATES" also know as the corporate DISTRICT UNITED STATES; or the "Federal Zone".

11 In 1935, the all capital letter printed-name Strawman — the newly created "artificial person" that has no brain and speaks and acts for its once-upon-a-time sovereign (*you and me*) — was created while Americans were distracted and confused by the introduction of *The New World Order* (*communistic socialism*) to figure out that they even *had* a Strawman with which to contend.

12 The Scarecrow identified this *strawman persona* for Dorothy thusly:

13 *"Some people without brains do an awful lot of talking. Of course; I'm not bright about doing things."*

14 In his classic song, *"If I Only Had A Brain,"* the Scarecrow/strawman succinctly augured, *"I'd unravel every riddle / For every Individdle / In trouble or in pain."*

15 Individual: a United States government *employee. (Title 5 USC §552(a)2).*

16 The Internal Revenue Code (IRC) and all State tax codes are in harmony with the above definition of *"individual"* by reference only.

17 A *"corporation-of-one"* is an artificial person constructed by law — a Strawman — not a living, breathing woman or man.

18 An *"individual"* is a public *corporate persona* existing only in the public domain (*government domain*) having been created by man's law instead of by God.

19 The drafters of codes and laws take everyday common speech and give it encrypted arcane meanings that are generally unknown or unknowable to the common man even after serious study.

20 Therefore, most folks are commercially, legally, and financially enslaved because of their ignorance of the truth.

21 Even while told that *"ignorance of the law is no excuse"* they find themselves helpless, unarmed, and uninformed.

22 Once we discover that our Strawman exists and that we have co-signed for him (it), all political and legal mysteries are resolved.

23 When we take title to our Strawman, we protect ourselves from any liabilities that we might otherwise occur.

24 The tin-man, our Taxpayer-Identification Number (TIN) man, is a hollow man of tin, a *vessel,* or *vehicle;* newly created code word*s* meaning our Strawman.

25 Just as the strawman has no brain, the tin-man vessel/vehicle has no heart; both are artificial persons. (*person = persona = mask*).

26 Persons are divided by law into natural and artificial.

27 Natural persons are persons created by God, and artificial persons are persons devised by human law for the purpose of governing them as *corporations-of-one* or bodies-politic.

28 The precise definition of the term "person" is therefore necessary to identify those to whom the 14th Amendment to the Constitution affords its protections and liabilities, since the 14th Amendment expressly applies to "persons."

29 A strawman is a person with a fictitious name written in *legalese* — language foreign to the rules of English grammar.

30 Men and women with names written in cursive — with initial-letters-only capitalized — are not "persons" even though they are referred to as natural persons, at times.

31 It is as impossible for a *person* to be natural as it is for a man to be artificial; "person" is a silent artificial construct hatched up by lawyers to be used and controlled by lawyers and their encrypted "codes."

32 One of the definitions of "tin" in Webster's dictionary is "counterfeit."

33 The Tin-man represents the mechanical and heartless aspect of commerce, and commercial law.

34 Just like they say in the Mafia as they throw you overboard, with your feet in cement, *"It's nothing personal; it's just business."*

35 The heartless Tin-man carried an "axe," a traditional symbol of modern commercial law in most dominant civilizations, including fascist states.

36 In the words of the "Tin-man" as he expressed relief after Dorothy had oiled his arm, *"I've held that axe up for ages."*

37 The word "ace" is etymologically related to the word "axe" and in a deck of cards the *only* card above the King is the Ace; meaning God.

38 One of the Axis Powers of World War II was a fascist state, Italy.

39 The symbol for fascism is the "fasces"; a bundle of rods with an axe bound up in it with the blade sticking out.

40 The "fasces" can be found on the reverse of the American Mercury-head dime (*the Roman deity, Mercury, is the God of*

Commerce) and on the wall behind and on each side of the Speaker's Podium in the United States House, each gold *fasces* being approximately six feet high.

41 At the base of the Seal of the United States House are two *fasces,* crossed.

42 *"IN GOD (MERCURY)(the God of Commerce) WE TRUST"* is printed on our Federal Reserve's one "dollar" bill.

43 The Cowardly-lion in the story represents the *at-one-time fearless* American people as having lost their courage.

44 And, after a round with the IRS, in "defending" your *TIN-man; dummy corporation; vehicle vessel; individual employee; public corporation; all capital letters written name; artificial person; Strawman,* you'd lose your courage too.

45 You perhaps haven't *known it,* but the IRS has been dealing with you all along *via your Tin-man* under the hidden laws of commerce.

46 Just like the *Tin-man,* "commerce" has no heart; "commerce" is heartless.

47 To find the Wizard, you have

to *"follow the yellow-brick road"* (*the gold-bar road*); follow the trail of America's stolen gold and you'll find the thief who stole it.

48 In the beginning of the Movie, the Wizard's counterpart was the traveling mystic, "Professor Marvel," who Dorothy encountered when she ran away with Toto.

49 His macabre shingle touted that he was *"acclaimed by The Crowned Heads of Europe, Past, Present, and Future."*

50 Professor Marvel must have *really* been a Wizard to be acclaimed so by the future Crowned Heads of Europe, even before they were crowned!

51 Before the Bankers stole America, they had long-since overpowered the Christian Kings and Queens of Europe and looted their kingdoms.

52 Maybe "Professor Marvel" knew something about the future that other folks didn't know.

53 With the *human skull* of a dead man peering down from its painted perch above the door to his wagon, the professor told Dorothy about the priests of Isis and Osiris, the Paraohs of Egypt,

and the days of yore.

54 When Dorothy Gale and her new friends emerged from the forest, they were elated to see the Emerald City before them, only a short distance away.

55 The Wicked Witch of the West, desperate for the ruby slippers that Dorothy was wearing, would have to *"make her move"* before our heroes arrived safely inside the Emerald City gates.

56 In the original book, *The Wonderful Wizard of Oz,* by Frank Baum, published 9 years before the Movie came out in 1939, and three years before the Crash, the slippers were not *red,* but *silver.*

57 America still had its gold in 1930, and the value of 1 oz. of gold was set at 15 ozs. of silver; silver being the more plentiful.

58 But when the Movie came out in 1939, the slippers were not *silver,* but *ruby-red.*

59 Between 1913 and 1933, America's gold was absorbed by the private non-federal Federal Reserve and shipped off to FED owners in England and Germany because the use of Federal Reserve Notes carried an interest penalty charge that could be paid only in gold.

60 Our *former* currency, United States Notes, carried no such interest penalty charge, but such was the so-called bargain "New Deal" that came with *"The New World Order"* of the non-federal Federal Reserve Act of 1913.

61 When the United States Bankruptcy was declared 20 years thereafter, in 1933, Americans were induced to *surrender* all their gold coin, gold bullion, and gold certificates by May 1st — *"May Day"* — the anniversary the birthday of Communism and the Illuminati in 1776, — the year that the American Colonists declared their independence from the Crown, on America's 4th of July.

62 Talking to people who were alive at that time, the general sentiment toward such "theft" in 1933, bordered on a Third Revolutionary War.

63 Maybe it was too much of a clue, or too much salt in their wounds, for Dorothy to be skipping down the golden yellow-brick road in a pair of silver slippers.

64 So, for whatever reason, a color less likely to provoke the

people was selected; *the color of Christ's sacrificial blood.*

65 With regard to the choice of ruby slippers — slippers colored red — another explanation is that on commercial documents and the like, *red signifies private as opposed to public.*

66 Your new Social Security Card has a *red serial number* on the reverse.

67 But no matter their color in the Movie, the Wicked Witch of the West had big plans to get her hands on the precious slippers before Dorothy and crew could make it to the Emerald City of Green paper *Federal Reserve Notes.*

68 The Wicked Witch of the West's tactic was to drug Dorithy into unconsciousness by covering the countryside with poppy flowers (poppies) — the source of *heroin, opium,* and *morphine* — and then waltz in and snatch the slippers.

69 In other words, the best way to loot the gold was to dull the senses of the American people with a *contrived crisis* (*the Great Depression*).

70 The poppy-drugs worked on Dorothy, the Lion and the dog Toto — the flesh-and-blood entities — but had no effect on the Scarecrow or the Tin-man — the artificial entities.

71 The Scarecrow and the Tin-man cried out for help, and Glenda — the Good Witch of the North — answered their cries with a blanket of snow that nullified the narcotic effect of the poppies on Dorothy, Toto, and the Lion.

72 As they all scampered toward the Emerald City — the city of green non-federal Federal Reserve Notes (*the new fiat money; paper money by decree*) — we hear the Munchkins singing the glories of the Wizard's Creation:

73 *"You're out of the woods / Your out of the dark / Your out of the night. / Step into the sun / Step into the light. / Keep straight ahead for the most glorious place / on the face of the earth or the stars!"*

74 This jingle abounds with *Illuminati-Luciferian* metaphors regarding darkness and light.

75 The Wicked Witch of the West made her home in a round medieval Watchtower — ancient symbol of The Knights Templar

of Freemasonry who are given to practicing witchcraft and are also credited to be *the originators of modern banking,* circa 1099 A.D.

76 The Wicked Witch of the West was dressed in black, the color that symbolizes the planet Saturn, a sacred icon of The Knights Templar, and "the color of choice" of judges and priests for their robes.

77 Who was the Wicked Witch of the West?

78 Remember, in the first part of the film her *counterpart* was Almira Gulch who according to Aunt Em *"owned half the county."*

79 Miss. Gulch claimed that Dorothy's dog, Toto, had bitten her.

80 She came to the farm with an *"order from the Sheriff"* demanding that they surrender Toto into her custody and control.

81 Aunt Em was not at first cooperative and answered Miss. Gulch's allegations that Toto had bitten her, *"He's really gentle; with gentle (Gentile) people, that is."*

82 When Miss. Gulch challenged them to withhold Toto from her and *"go against the law,"* dear old Aunt Em was relegated (*committed*) to "pushing the Party Line" for Big Brother government.

83 Aunt Em dutifully succumbed to the pressure and counselled Dorothy, reluctantly, *"We can't go against the law, Dorothy. I'm afraid poor Toto will have to go."*

84 When Dorothy refused to surrender Toto, Miss Gulch lashed out:

85 *"If you don't hand over that dog I'll bring a suit that'll take your whole farm!"*

86 Today 70% of all attorneys in the world reside in the West — in America to be exact — and 95% of all law suites in the world are filed under the Jurisdiction of the corporate UNITED STATES.

87 The Wicked Witch of the West and Miss. Gulch symbolize Judges and Attorneys — primary agents for the transfer of all wealth in America from the People to the United States, the United Nations, and the International Banks.

88 The American Bar Association is a branch of the Bar Coun-

cil under the Bar Association of England and Wales.

89 As the copyrighted property of a British Company, all States' and United States' Codes are *private British owned Law,* and all States' and United States' Courts, state Bar Associations, and the "STATE OF *each of the 50 States*" go by and enforce *private British owned Law* against Americans, operating as *private foreign owned tribunals or administrative agencies* doing business in the States under the cover and color of each of the 50 states' law.

90 The Wicked Witch of the West wanted the ruby (*silver*) slippers (*the precious metals*) — and her counterpart Miss. Gulch, wanted Toto too.

91 What does "toto" signify in attorney legalese? "Everything!" Miss. Gulch wanted to take everything.

92 Dorothy and the gang fell for *the Wizard's illusion,* in the beginning, but soon wised up and discovered the Wizard for what he was; a confidence man.

93 When asked about helping the Scarecrow/strawman, the Wizard — among his *babblings*

about *getting a brain* and *universities* — cited the land of "E Pluribus Unum" (*Latin for "One out of many" or converting many into one*) meaning The New World Order.

94 "Novus Ordo Seclorum" (*The New World Order*) is the Latin phrase placed on the American one-dollar bill shortly after the Bankruptcy of the U.S. Government was declared in 1933.

95 The Wizard proudly *confessed* that he was, *"Born and bred in the heart of the western wilderness; an old Kansas man myself."*

96 The Bankers did quite well.

97 They, as the Wizard said, made a killing in the American West with their theft of America's gold, labor, and property from the *"grateful and responsive rural folk"* (*a quoted phrase of John D. Rocke-feller*) who populated the country farms at that time.

98 When Dorothy asked Glenda, the Good Witch of the North for her help in getting back to Kansas, Glenda replied...

99 *"You don't need to be helped; you've always had the*

power to go back to Kansas."

100 Translation: You've always had the right and power to re-claim your sovereignty; you just forgot your remedy — a UCC-1 Form and Security Agreement sent to the Secretary of State and an Invoice and Bill of Exchange sent to the Secretary of the U.S. Treasury, that can be completed from scratch in a very short time.

101 Remedy: Remedy is the means by which the violation of a right is prevented, redressed, or compensated.

102 Both remedy and rights include those remedial rights of self-help which are among the most important bodies of rights under the Universal Commercial Code (UCC).

103 Remedial rights are rights that an aggrieved party can resort to on his own.

104 "Acceptance of Value" is our Remedy.

105 Americans have intimate firsthand knowledge of the heartless mechanics of the laws of commerce when strictly applied by the *unregistered, foreign agents* of the IRS.

106 The Internal Revenue Service is the collection agency for the private non-federal Federal Reserve Bank and the International Monetary Fund.

107 The IRS was placed under the Uniform Commercial Code in 1954 and has been operating strictly in that realm ever since.

108 You may have wondered about the meaning behind the words *The Wizard of Oz*. Look them up in the dictionary. Like almost everything else, the *ruse* is out in the open for all to see, if you will but look and see.

109 One definition of *Wizard* is *"a person of high professional knowledge or skill."*

110 *Oz* is an abbreviation of "onza," the Italian word for ounce (oz.), the unit of measurement of silver and gold and other precious metals.

111 No matter how large the quantity of gold or silver being discussed, the amount is always expressed in *ounces* rather than hundreds of tons of gold, its stated as so many million ounces of gold.

112 Everything worked out for Dorothy (*the American people*) in the end. In the end, Dorothy *"made it home"* to Kansas and

her friends.

113 Translation: There's a Remedy encoded, disguised, and camouflaged in law. The UCC has been cracked and there's a way home, just like in the Movie.

114 Like Dorothy said, *"There's no place like home"* — there's no status like sovereignty for a sovereign!

115 Admiralty courts are courts established in the Queen's possessions beyond the seas, having jurisdiction over maritime causes and those relating to prize.

116 The United States is a *colony* of the English Crown per *a joint venture commercial agreement between the united States and the Crown,* that brought the United States back under British possession and rule.

117 But the American People had "standing in law" as sovereigns; *independent of any connection to the United States and the Crown.*

118 This sovereignty required that the People be quietly brought back under British rule, *one at a time.*

119 And CPR — *the Commercial Process of Redemption via the UCC* — will redeem us from this ruse.

120 Will you continue to be conned by confidence men into worshiping the Wizard's light-show (the Apocalypse Beast) or will you *look behind the veil?*s

CHAPTER 35

THE *one aim of the financiers is world control, by the creation of inextinguishable debt."* — *Henry Ford.*

2 Since 1933, all Americans have been pledged for the debt that the federal UNITED STATES owes to international bankers, most of whom are foreign to this country.

3 Your credit, property and labor have been pledged as collateral for the national debt of the corporate UNITED STATES — without your knowledge or consent.

4 This is *legal* until you redeem (*take back*) your *implied consent* by a special process of law.

5 You have unknowingly *volunteered* to be chattel for a mortgage held by financiers, from the founding of this nation.

6 To finance the War of Independence from the King of England, the thirteen American Colonies borrowed money from the Crown; 3,000,000 livres in 1778; 1,000,000 livres in 1779; 4,000,000 livres in 1780; and 6,000,000 livres in 1782 — for a total of 18,000,000 livres in all.

7 *See the Contract between the King and the thirteen United States of North America, signed at Versailles, France, July 16, 1782.*

8 Perhaps you *assume* that the name on the tax statements and bills that you receive is your name, and so you respond as if it were.

9 *This is voluntary servitude.*

10 To make this *voluntary servitude* legal it was necessary to *"cut a hole in the fence"* so to speak.

11 It doesn't matter that the escape route is hidden by legal brambles to make escape difficult.

12 Your *not* using the "remedy" provided, *presumes* your consent.

13 It is not impossible to escape, just seemingly difficult — and *implausible,* to boot.

14 Your status as a subject of the democracy is based upon the *presumption* that if you did not wish to be so encumbered by *voluntary servitude* you would use the law provided to do something about it.

15 As long as you do not use the *"remedy"* provided by law,

it is *presumed* that you are content to remain in the pasture and be used as *chattel* for the federal debt.

16 This word *"chattel"* has the same root as the word *"cattle"*; get the picture?

17 *Can such a premise be true?*

18 It seems completely out of step with everything you and I have ever learned about our world, our nation, our government; and our relationship to it!

19 Our parents never behaved as though they we were chattel. Did they? They dutifully paid their taxes, voted in elections, and waved an American flag on the 4th of July.

20 Our school teachers taught us about our history; our Declaration of Independence and the Constitution of our Republic; our Revolutionary War; how we fought the greatest army and navy that the world had ever seen at the time.

21 Nowhere in our history classes did we encounter any such premise of subjection to the central government that rules our lives today.

22 Our Civics teachers never told us anything about this.

23 Nothing in our world even hinted that we are the *subjects* of a highly centralized government.

24 Surely this might be true of other peoples in other lands, but *not* of us here in America!

25 For most intelligent Americans, this simply "cannot be".

26 The truth *cannot be heard* because it is too much in discord with our entire experience.

27 Do not take the expression *"cannot be heard"* as just a figure of speech. In practical conversation this turns out to be literally true.

28 Either a person will miss what is being said, entirely, or if he hears it at all, he will argue — fight the concept — refuse to hear it.

29 If you are an exception, count yourself *OPEN MINDED* and *blessed.*

30 You have in your vision, right now, the knowledge that can help you to escape this tragic situation.

31 We can now document that George Washington did *not* chop down a cherry tree;

32 ...that Lincoln did *not* free the slaves (they became subjects

of the Federal District; the District of Columbia);

33 ...that Zachary Taylor's provocations along the Nueces River started the War with Mexico;

34 ...that the battleship *Maine* blew up *from the inside;*

35 ...that Woodrow Wilson *knew* that the *Lusitania* was carrying US munitions to the war in Europe and *would be sunk;*

36 ...that Franklin D. Roosevelt *maneuvered* the Japanese into an attack on Pearl Harbor, and cut off fuel shipments to the Pacific fleet to ensure the presence of enough old ships to offer a tempting target to the Japanese;

37 ...that Harry Truman *knew* that there were other good alternatives to an invasion of Japan and that he did *not* need to drop the Atomic Bomb on Hiroshima and Nagasaki;

38 ...that Roosevelt *knew* about the NAZI concentration camps;

39 ...that L.B.J. *knew* that there was no attack on the *Maddox and Turner Joy* in the Gulf of Tonkin when he asked for a Congressional Resolution to attack North Vietnam;

40 ...and that the US government had been *warned* by numerous documented sources that there would be an attack on the *World Trade Center* and the *Pentagon,* on 9/11 (2001).

41 All of this is from documented historical sources; yet we continue to believe the *myths* in our histories, our movies, our mainstream media, and our mass consciousness.

42 President John F Kennedy warned us:

43 ***"The great enemy of the Truth is very often not the lie — deliberate, contrived and dishonest — but the myth — persistent, persuasive and seemingly real."***

44 You will probably find it hard to accept that you have been living in an *illusion* for your whole life.

45 Much of what you believe is an *illusion,* and you will only find your freedom when you can allow yourself to *look behind the veil,* and see reality.

46 May the grace of our Lord Jesus Christ be with you all. Amen.

CHAPTER 36

THE government isn't based on truth; the government is based on **agreement contracts**.

2 If we were to list all of the God-given freedoms that we have voluntarily *exchanged* for government privileges we would fill a number of pages.

3 We have been trapped by our ignorance of the law, despite being told early in life, that *"ignorance of the law is no excuse"*.

4 Once we start doing business with Caesar — *willingly giving him what is God's* — we find ourselves locked into a web of *presumptive* and *expressed* contracts.

5 A key point to understand is this:

6 There are no limits in law to what two parties can agree to by contract as long as it does not harm a third party.

7 So if you agree to give all your property to another party, or to be treated in any way that party may deem best, there is nothing in law to which you can appeal should you later discover that you've been wronged.

8 Caesar's modern State is just such a contractual relationship with one key difference: we were never told we were *contracting* our God-given freedoms away as a result of government fraud.

9 First: It is an all or nothing contract; if you agree to one part of the contract you agree to the whole thing.

10 So Christians who have been mis-taught, who think they should go along with the statutes of the State out of obedience to Scripture — are giving legitimacy to *all* the godless actions of the State. We were told that we had no choice but to accept the *all* because *"it's the law"*.

11 However, we now see that this is *"not the law"* at all. But simply a *contractual relationship* with the State. And as such, the contract can be terminated.

12 Second: At its root this contract involves the payment of debts we never agreed to.

13 We have been sold into bondage by fraud, and unless something changes we will sell our children and grandchildren into this same ever worsening *delusion,* for *"a mess of pottage"*.

14 Third: The scriptural solution is to *"come out of her, my*

people". (Revelation 18:4; II Corinthians 6:17).

15 This does not mean coming out of the nation or violating its laws. These laws are still consistent with the Law of God and are what Scripture refers to when telling us to obey legitimate earthly authority.

16 However, when we obey judges and police officers who are sworn to uphold *legitimate laws,* but are in fact enforcing *illegitimate statutes,* we become *party* to their evil, in neither upholding *legitimate laws* nor honoring God.

17 We devote our energies to obeying *the whims of men* which change over night and grow increasingly depraved.

18 It is the statutory, contract laws of the State that we must stop trying to *"fix"* and instead *"rebut"* and *"reject"* — and no longer honor and uphold.

19 May the grace of our Lord Jesus Christ be with you all. Amen.

CHAPTER 37

NOW that you understand the structure of modern law, you are ready to see how perfectly Scripture described the modern system in America thousands of years in advance.

2 Most aware Christians are waiting for the day when a computer chip will be implanted in their forehead or in their hand.

3 At that time, they will make a decision to accept the chip or reject it.

4 What they do not realize is that we have already accepted the mark of the beast.

5 *"And he causeth all, both small and great, rich and poor, free and bond, to receive a mark in their right hand, or in their foreheads: And that no man might buy or sell, save he that had the mark, or the name of the beast, or the number of his name."* — *Revelation 13:16-17.*

6 First note that there is not just a *mark* but also a *name* and a *number.*

7 What does the State always need from you?

8 The *artificial-person's name* and *social security number* and *birth date.*

9 We have to love the Canadians who call the *social security number* a *social insurance number; SIN* instead of SSN.

10 We cannot do business with the State without *these three things,* nor can we open a bank account or access other conveniences of modern society without *these three things.*

11 It becomes more impossible each year to buy and sell without the *mark,* the *name* and the *number* of the beast.

12 But the *Real Mark* is the kicker that has been sitting there in Scripture all along.

13 *"And it shall be for a sign unto thee upon thine hand, and for a memorial between thine eyes, that God's law may be in thy mouth."* — *Exodus 13:9.*

14 This is repeated in one of the most famous passages of the Old Testament:

15 *"Hear, O Israel: The Lord our God is one Lord: And thou shalt love the Lord thy God with all thine heart, and with all thy soul, and with all thy might.*

16 *"And these words, which I command thee this day, shall be in thine heart: And thou shalt teach them diligently unto thy*

children, and shalt talk of them when thou sittest in thine house, and when thou walkest by the way, and when thou liest down, and when thou risest up.

17 *"And thou shalt bind them for a <u>sign upon thine hand</u>, and they shall be as <u>frontlets between thine eyes</u>.*

18 *"And thou shalt write them upon the posts of thy house, and on thy gates."* — *Deuteronomy 6:4-9.*

19 What is supposed to be already in our hand and in our forehead (*between thine eyes*)? — *God's Law!*

20 If God's Law is there, how could the beast's counterfeit MARK take its place?

21 The modern church has neglected God's Law in the name of being *"Not under law, but under grace."*

22 In its place we have accepted the beast's *statute law* as his *mark.*

23 Because people no longer think of Law as something fixed or unchanging, the church misses the blessings of having an *unchanging* Law to follow; and accepts in its place the burden of *ever-changing* statutes.

24 "Grace" is taught as being the *opposite* of Law, when the *true biblical opposite* of Law is "iniquity"; or "lawlessness".

25 How many Christians "under grace" are in fact living "in iniquity?"

26 Our failure to understand leads the church to teach that obedience to *ever-changing statutes* is what Peter and Paul had in mind when they told us to submit to earthy authorities.

27 Yet these *ever-changing statutes* are contradictory to, and a replacement for the *Law of God.*

28 This is precisely what Daniel saw several millennia ago while in Babylon:

29 *"Thus he said, The fourth beast shall be the fourth kingdom upon earth, which shall be diverse from all kingdoms, and shall <u>devour the whole earth</u>, and shall tread it down, and <u>break it in pieces</u>.*

30 *"And he shall speak great words against the most High, and shall <u>wear out the saints</u> of the most High, and think to <u>change times and laws</u>: and they shall be given into his hand until a time and times and the di-*

viding of time." — Daniel 7:23, 25.

31 The modern church has already embraced the *mark,* the *name* and the *number* of the beast — and continues to tell its members to do so as good Christians.

32 Most Christians are busily and unknowingly rendering unto Caesar, in the name of obedience to God, the things that should rightfully be rendered unto God.

33 Caesar has usurped God's authority — and Caesar's kingdom is being built with our consent by using legal fictions in our behalf.

34 *Caesar's authority over us is imaginary.*

35 We do not have to render ourselves as slaves unto Caesar unless we believe that we belong to him.

36 Commercial Redemption, like Spiritual Redemption is *also* a part of God's Plan.

37 May the grace of our Lord Jesus Christ be with you all. Amen.

CHAPTER 38

THE Federal Reserve is a private company of bankers consisting of twelve branch banks designed to confiscate our wealth; and they have been doing this for nearly one hundred years.

2 These banks are not part of the United States Government, yet today they collect hundreds of billions of dollars from American taxpayers each year in the biggest and most successful scam in History.

3 Meyer Amschel Rothschild (1743-1812) said, *"Let me issue and control a nation's money, and I care not who writes its laws."*

4 It was Alexander Hamilton who lobbied for the first privately owned non-federal Federal Bank, and Congress chartered this bank in 1789.

5 In 1811, President Thomas Jefferson refused to renew the charter for the bank stating, *"I sincerely believe that the banking institutions, having the issuing power of money, are more dangerous to liberty than standing armies."*

6 In 1816 Congress established the second non-federal Federal Bank, but in 1836, President Andrew Jackson overrode Congress and closed it commenting,

7 *"The bold efforts the present bank had made to control the government are but premonitions of the fate that awaits the American people should they be deluded into a perpetuation of this institution or the establishment of another like it."* (We now have another like it).

8 Andrew Jackson also said, when speaking to the bankers: *"You are a den of vipers and thieves. I intend to rout you out, and by the grace of the eternal God, I will rout you out."*

9 When speaking to his closest friend, Martin Van Buren, Jackson said, *"The bank, is trying to kill me, but I will kill it!* (they tried; and he did).

10 The first two Federal Reserve Systems lasted about 20 years each, and we are now nearly one hundred years into the third one.

11 As soon as Woodrow Wilson was elected president of the United States in 1913, he signed the *Federal Reserve Act* in return for financial support in be-

ing elected.

12 In December of 1913, the *Federal Reserve Act* was rammed through Congress while many members of Congress were home for the Christmas holiday.

13 Wilson admitted at a later date, with remorse, when referring to the fed, *"I have unwittingly ruined my country"!*

14 We never had nor did we ever need an *income tax* until we got the bankers back as the Fed.

15 The *income tax* is only needed to pay interest to the bankers for the money that we use that they *loan* to our government.

16 Yes, you read that right, the Fed, mostly on paper and via computer entries, creates money, at a small printing fee for currency, and *loans* this money to our government at interest.

17 Our taxes pay the interest on this loan that costs the Fed virtually nothing to make; what a sweetheart of a deal they have going for them.

18 As of March 6, 2006, the national debt stands at 8.2 trillion dollars.

19 The American taxpayers have paid the Federal Reserve Banking System $173,875,979,369 in interest on that debt in just the five short months, from October, 2005, through February, 2006.

20 No con artist or group of con artists in history has ever perpetrated such a scam that even approaches the scope of this one mentioned here.

21 According to the two volume work by Bill Benson and Red Beckman — *"The Law That Never Was"*— the 16th amendment, which created the IRS, was never ratified, even by one state!

22 These two gentlemen traveled the then 48 states to verify that fact!

23 So in a very real sense, the income tax is not legal — as many have proclaimed — but try not paying it after you have *voluntarily* filed a *perjured* return, and see how far you get before the Feds come after you and confiscate everything you own.

24 Henry Ford once said, *"It is well enough that people of the nation do not understand our banking and monetary system, for if they did, I believe there would be a revolution before tomorrow morning."*

25 In nearly 100 years of the existence of the fed, it has NEVER been audited and these banks do not pay income tax on the billions of dollars they take from us.

26 According to Congressional record, the U.S. Government can buy back the Fed at any time for $450 million dollars.

27 This is about half of the amount of money we pay them each day.

28 Do we have the most stupid and or corrupt leaders in the world — or what?

29 It seems that their number one concern is getting re-elected.

30 Congress likes the Fed because they can spend all that they want with no restraints, they just put our children, grandchildren and great-grandchildren into un-payable debt.

31 A Federal Reserve note is just what it looks like, it is just a piece of paper with no backing at all.

33 Article 1, section 8, clause 5 of the Constitution of the United States reads: *"The Congress shall have the Power... To coin money, [and] regulate the value thereof..."*

34 Nowhere in that document does the Constitution give Congress the authority to delegate this responsibility to anyone; much less to a private bankers' cartel.

35 President John F. Kennedy had the foresight to see what a bad deal had been struck in the creation of the non-federal Federal Reserve.

36 Kennedy had the courage to do something about it, which unfortunately, cost him his life.

37 On June 4, 1963, President Kennedy signed Presidential, Executive Order 1110.

38 This order virtually stripped the Federal Reserve Bank of its power to loan money to the United States at interest.

39 President Kennedy predicted that the privately owned Federal Reserve Bank would soon be out of business.

40 This order gave the Treasury Department the authority to issue silver certificates against any silver in the treasury.

41 This executive order still stands today.

42 In less than five months after signing that executive order, President Kennedy was assassi-

nated on November 22, 1963.

43 The United States Notes (*silver certificates*) he had issued were taken out of circulation at once; while Federal Reserve Notes continued to serve as the legal currency of this nation.

44 It is estimated that 99% of all U.S. paper currency circulating today are Federal Reserve Notes.

45 Abraham Lincoln also took on the bankers, and that brave, bold step likewise cost him his life.

46 During the civil War (1861-1865) President Lincoln needed money to finance the war for the North.

47 The bankers were going to charge him 24% to 36% interest.

48 Lincoln was horrified; and he refused to plunge the country that he loved into a debt that the country could never pay back.

49 So Lincoln advised Congress to pass a law authorizing the printing of *full legal tender Treasury notes* to pay for the War effort.

50 Lincoln recognized the great benefits of this issue.

51 At one point, Lincoln wrote,

"...[we] gave the people of this Republic the greatest blessing they have ever had, their own paper money to pay their own debts..."

52 The Treasury notes were printed with green ink on the back, so the people called them *"Greenbacks"*.

53 Lincoln printed 400 million dollars worth of *Greenbacks,* money that he delegated to be created — a debt-free and interest-free money to finance the Civil War.

54 It served as legal tender for all debts, public and private.

55 Lincoln printed it, paid it to the soldiers, to U.S. Civil service employees, and bought supplies for the war.

56 Lincoln was assassinated shortly after the war and Congress revoked the greenback law and enacted, the national Banking Act in its place.

57 The national banks were to be privately owned and the national bank notes they issued were to bear interest.

58 The Act *also* provided that the *Greenbacks* should be retired from circulation as soon as they came back to the Treasury in

payment of taxes.

59 When you follow the money you find that no-one in the world had a better reason to kill these two Presidents than the bankers.

60 It is inconceivable that anyone could think there was no conspiracy in the assassination of JFK, especially when you consider the many people who were murdered or had suspicious deaths, who were associated with Kennedy's assassination in some way.

61 Is this proof? NO...

62 Is this strong *circumstantial evidence?* YOU DECIDE!

63 *The Federal Reserve, United Nations, Council on Foreign Relations, Trilateral Commission, the Illuminati, the Bilderbergers,* and other elites of the hidden government, are leading us into *The New World Order* and they are leading us fast.

64 Only we the people can save this Republic!

65 May the grace of our Lord Jesus Christ be with you all. Amen.

High Flight

Oh! I have slipped the surely bonds of earth
  And danced the skies on laughter-silvered wings.

Sunward I've climbed,
  And joined the tumbling mirth Of sun-split clouds,
    And done a hundred things you have not
      dreamed of.

Wheeled and soared and swung high in the sunlit
  silence;

  And while — with silent lifting mind, —
    I've trod the high, untrespassed sanctity of
space —

  Put out my hand, — and touched the face of God.

John Gillespie Magee

EPISTLE TO THE AMERICANS I
What you don't know about the Income Tax

EPISTLE TO THE AMERICANS II
What you don't know about American History

EPISTLE TO THE AMERICANS III
What you don't know about Money

Made in the USA